Careby

Carlb

Effendine

House

Toltho....

Little
Casterton

STAMFORD

St Martins

SHIR

LA

JOHN CARY

Statute Miles 69½

A
Celebration
of
Rutland

Sponsored by Ruddles Brewery, Langham

Rutland
Youth Band
celebrate at
the Oakham
Festival

A
Celebration
of
Rutland

Edited by Bryan Waites
Designed by Philip Dawson

MULTUM
IN PARVO
PRESS
Oakham, Rutland
1994

Published by Multum in Parvo Press
6 Chater Road, Oakham, Rutland LE15 6RY

©

All rights reserved.

ISBN 0 9524544 0 8

A Celebration of Rutland 1994
has been published in a Limited Edition
of which this is

Number

886

A list of patrons and subscribers is given
at the end of the book.

Printed in England
by Warwick Printing Company Limited
Theatre Street, Warwick CV34 4DR

Contents

HISTORY

ARTS

COMMUNITY

Contributors

Richard Adams
Philip Dawson
Gerald Botteley
Margaret Towl
Bryan Waites
Rutland Natural History Society
   Irvine Cushing
   James Eaton
   Philip Rudkin Chairman
   Graham Worrall
   George Sellars
   Linda Worrall
   Patrick Mann
   Jean Harvey
   Ray Butchart
   Ron Harvey
   Dr Anthony Fletcher
   Jenny Harris
   R E Stebbings
   M Frankum
   S Dalton
   M Boulton
   Barbara Parker
   Michael Iannantuoni
Hilary Burn
Alan Pimperton
   and students of Vale of Catmose
   College, Oakham
Andrew Jenkins
Robert Ovens
Derek Griffiths
Dr Trevor Bell
June Lawton
T H McK Clough,
   Keeper Rutland County Museum
Carl Harrison,
   County Archivist and Staff of the
   Leicestershire Record Office
K W Weatherhogg
Professor L M Cantor
Anne-Marie Evans
Dr Donn Evans
Geoff Hamilton
Stephen Hamilton
Tim Appleton, Warden Rutland
   Water Nature Reserve
Carol Debney

David Moore,
   Recreation Manager Anglian Water
Gordon Langsbury
Sheila Sleath
Nicholas Meadwell
Eddie Hudson, Editor Rutland Times
Richard Clarke
Ian Balfour
Brian Hollingshead
Roger Blackmore
J Rudman
David Gaine
J P W Metcalfe
RAF Cottesmore
   Fl Lieut Andy Harwood
   N J Roberson
   J G Tallis
RAF North Luffenham
   Fl Lieut Maggie Fish
Richard Knight
   and Rutland Railway Museum
Peter Smith
T Weeden
Sgt Major Warren, Uppingham School
Rutland Times
Woodland Trust
John Barber
Sarah Linden, Bev Craven
   and Rutland Design Co Oakham
Justine Fosh and Ruddles Brewery
Lady Ruddle
Tony Ruddle
Geoffrey R Herrickx
Rigby Graham
Alan Oliver
Trevor Hickman
Penny & John Richardson
Sharon Broome
David Millard
David Carlin
Canon John Prophet
Dr Philip Ennis
Kathleen McKinnon
John Crossley
Derek Harrison
   and the Stamford Shakespeare
   Company, Rutland Theatre

Editorial Team

Bryan Waites
Philip Dawson
Eddie Hudson
Carol Debney

Acknowledgements

The Editor is grateful to all contributors and apologises in the event of any names being inadvertently omitted above. He also appreciates the co-operation of Anglian Water, Leicester Mercury, Rutland Mercury, Mrs Hoy, Mike Goldmark, Brian and Elizabeth Nicholls, Leicestershire Museum Arts and Records Service, the Station Commanders RAF Cottesmore and North Luffenham, the Headmasters and Trustees of Oakham and Uppingham Schools, Pan Macmillan, London and Ian Crofton, Trout Fishing and Country Walking magazines, Savill International Stamford Office, the British Boxing Board of Control, Rutland Historic Churches Trust, Lady Campden and Spiegl Press and many others too numerous to name. The considerable help and co-operation given surely, in itself alone, indicates the true spirit of Rutland.

Introduction

When Abraham Lincoln gave his Gettysburg Address in 1863, the last thing on his mind was Rutland, England. Indeed, it is likely that he had never heard of it. Yet, his memorable words, delivered 3000 miles away, touch very closely on the Spirit of Rutland. Why is Rutland so special? What exactly is the Spirit of Rutland?

Both questions are not easy to answer, but it is certain that somewhere in the definition there is the notion of independence within a small area for more than 1000 years duration, including active participation of the whole community in the government of the area. That is, the concept of a personal possession, but for a whole community.

Much has been written about Rutland's distinctiveness as this passage shows:

Everyone may have heard of Rutland, after all it was England's smallest county but how many had been there? Probably very few and those who had may have passed through only on the A1. Would they have found something special if they had lingered?

At least in the right spot they could see across the county, a distance of only 17 miles. This was in keeping with the county motto Multum in Parvo, much from little.

This small county in the heart of the English Shires was a microcosm of rural England. Gently undulating but unspectacular landscape with good arable land in the east and well-wooded pastureland in the west. Quiet, winding, half-hidden country lanes led to brown-stone villages and sleepy market towns.

There was little hint of industry except for the eternal chimneys of Ketton Cement Works on the far horizon.

In Oakham and Uppingham, built to a formula it seemed, could be found church, school, market place and High Street in close companionship. The former marked its county town status by the 12th century Castle Hall full of lordly horseshoes given for 1000 years by visiting Peers of the Realm. It had its Assize Court and close by, its Butter Cross.

There were too, the stately homes, great public schools and the Cottesmore Hunt contributing to the personality of Rutland. Truly the county seemed an island of Stilton Cheese, Hunt Cakes, County Ale, Ketton Stone and Collyweston Slates, still largely untouched, still a picture of a human, peaceful slow-moving, pre-industrial England with seemly villages, handsome churches, great arable fields and barns......150 square miles of unknown England.

Rutland Record No 1, 1980

Cottage formerly at Lower Hambleton, drawn by Brian Hollingshead

Rutland has survived, just like Normanton Tower has survived – and that is why we have it on our front cover. There are more than 80 contributors to this book and they all believe that Rutland is special. They have combined here to prove it. Many organisations and individuals show what is best about our natural environment, history, community and the arts. They do so in their own way. The emphasis is on visual presentation and the reader can let the book fall open almost anywhere to gain an appreciation of Rutland.

The book does not attempt to be exhaustive or comprehensive; nor does it include everything or everyone who might have been featured, but we hope the selection is good enough to provide a permanent record of Rutland in the past and the present. It is our belief that this record so provided can help us all to cherish our inheritance better, to recognise it clearly and to love it more dearly.

Bryan Waites

Abroad Thoughts From Home

You can have the sands of Morocco
Or the burning sun of Greece,
I'll let you stew
By Pacific blue
And the waving palms of Nice.

You can ride the droop-nosed Concorde
Or the Orient Express,
You may sail the Nile
In Cleo style
Or by Cyprus shores digress

I wish you well
Where the breakers swell
By a sun-kissed coral reef,
You can climb the Alps and the Rockies
And have views beyond belief.

I'll have respect
If you select
A Mediterranean cruise,
Nor criticise
If you think it wise
These distant sights to muse.

I'll just bless the rain
And not complain
While you sail the seven seas,
No I'll not roam
From native home
In Rutland I'm at ease.

by Eddie Hudson

**Sketches by
David Millard
Top: Braunston
Above: Barrow
Left: Teigh**

*This book is dedicated to
Mrs Winifred Clark and Mr John L. Barber
in recognition of their great services
to Rutland*

RUTLAND

8

A Wet Wood

Grey Squirrel.
Very common
where a few trees
grow, providing
shelter and food.
It eats a wide
range of food
from fruits and
berries to young
birds and insects.

Woodcock breed in Rutland and move in to local woods during the winter months. When they are sitting they rely on their colouring to protect them.

Prior's Coppice is one of the few remaining ancient woodlands in Rutland which has not been planted with conifers. Large rides allow in light and a moisture-retentive clay soil encourages a variety of flowers and grasses. The wide diversity of plants then provides food for the birds, insects and animals which use the wood as a refuge. With its increasingly rare habitat and wildlife abundance, the 70 acre wood was purchased in 1987 by Leicestershire and Rutland Trust for Nature Conservation and is managed as a Nature Reserve.

Right: Tawny Owl, the most common of our local owls. The female will lay between two and four eggs each year. The number of young to survive will depend on how much food the adult male can catch.

Below: Seven Spot Ladybirds. They are active from early spring to autumn and then look for a dry warm spot behind the bark of a tree to spend the cold winter months.

Below: Willow Warblers. One of the earliest migrants to return from Africa to find a mate, lay their eggs, raise a family and then return to Africa for the winter.

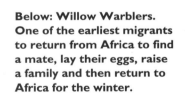

Ponds that are free of pollution are becoming scarce for frogs to live in and raise the next generation of tadpoles.

Dragonflies also need water that is unpolluted in which to breed. Their larvae can spend several years in ponds before emerging into a beautiful dragonfly like the Southern Hawker.

Water Avens. One of about 230 species of plant growing in this wood. Flowers are becoming scarcer due to draining and grassland improvement, but here they can flourish.

Text and photographs by Irvine Cushing, Rutland Natural History Society

Red Admiral Butterfly

Drinker Moth

Garden Wildlife

Robin, the 'national bird' of Britain, one of the gardener's most helpful allies in taking harmful insects to feed to their family during spring and summer.

Rutland gardens come in many shapes and sizes, varying in the type and range of habitat they provide for wildlife of all kinds. Like Nature Reserves, gardens are becoming a refuge against pollution and land improvement. It is an indication of their importance that the area of gardens in Rutland is greater than that of our Nature Reserves.

Insects visit our gardens both by day and night, relying on plants to supply their food. They themselves may become food for some of our garden birds! Birds which frequent our gardens range from rare species such as the Hobby to common birds like the Blackbird. To feed this variety of life we need to grow different plants and shrubs which give both choice and quantity.

Blackbird, juvenile

Guelder Rose

Left: Long Tailed Field Mouse. When the first frosts of autumn arrive, mice will move in to garden sheds for warmth and food.

Hobby, juvenile

Female Pheasants sit very tight when incubating eggs, but if disturbed reveal beautifully coloured eggs.

Honeysuckle

Head of a male Kestrel

Text and photographs by Irvine Cushing, Rutland Natural History Society

**Inset: Dark Bush
Cricket** *Pholidoptera
griseoaptera).* **This species is
found in all areas of Burley Wood
and is active in late summer and through the autumn
when its quiet stridulations can be heard during the
day, but especially during the evening when these
super little insects enjoy their evening chorus.**

Burley

Eight Riding Tree. A deer hide now stands where once the famous Eight Riding Tree graced the scene. It is here that eight rides meet, and where one can view the wildlife and rest awhile.

Photographs by James Eaton and Irvine Cushing. Text by Philip Rudkin, Chairman, Rutland Natural History Society

Burley House. This is the most famous Rutland landmark. Burley House stands proud at the top of a hill. Surviving all attempts to alter the outer appearance, this scene with the rich woodland flanking the approach, can be seen from the A606, and it is hoped that long may it remain so.

Bluebell (*Hyacinthoides non scripta*). Breathtaking in their beauty, this species carpets the woodland floor in April and early May. When the sun is 'dappling' through the trees, a sea of blue appears which is unsurpassed throughout Rutland.

ENVIRONMENT

Wood survives

Left: Great Spotted Woodpecker (*Dendrocopos major*). **This exciting woodpecker haunts the upper canopy in its search for wood boring grubs. Its nest sites are excavated in dead and dying parts of the trunks of trees. It is a successful breeding species in Burley Wood. The fascinating territorial drumming of this woodpecker rings out in the spring and is an integral part of the sounds of the woodland.**

Right:
Marsh Tit *(Parus palustris)*. **One of the six resident tit species to inhabit Burley Wood, a successful breeder in tree holes. In winter foraging flocks roam the areas searching for food.**

Left: A typical ride in Burley Wood, showing the mixed habitat and tree species to be found deep in the wood.

Below: Badger *(Meles meles)*. **One of Rutland's best known and well loved mammals. If seen it is quite unmistakable with its white head and conspicuous dark stripe on either side.**

Nuthatch *(Sitta europaea)*. **Another bird that shares the upper canopy with the woodpeckers and similar lifestyle. This species can walk up and down and sideways along branch or trunk, which is quite remarkable to observe. A superb range of call notes and song phrases can be heard throughout the wood in spring and summer.**

Left: Fox *(Vulpes vulpes)*. **A Rutland mammal that gives rise to mixed feelings and heated debate among the populace. However, the sight of a vixen playing with her cubs in a woodland setting is hard to resist. The autumn screaming of this species in the dark of night is a feature of the Rutland countryside.**

ENVIRONMENT

A Haven for Flowers?

Farming methods have changed drastically in the last 60 years and as a consequence most flower-rich pasture has been ploughed or improved. A few remnants exist, such as the Leicestershire and Rutland Trust for the Nature Conservation's Reserve at Merry's Meadows, Greetham, and a few SSSI sites scattered throughout Rutland.

Verges are perhaps the only remaining evidence of how varied Rutland's wild flowers were just three generations ago. Even now these beautiful flowers are in danger, the two main threats being so-called improved roads and the use of incorrect treatment. Too often verges are treated as garden lawns and too frequent mowing will eventually lead to the loss of the flowers.

There is still enough in the grassland ribbons we call verges to interest and fascinate those who are prepared to get out of their cars and stroll the varied verges of Rutland.

Above: Cow Parsley near Preston, April. Right: Bee Orchid, April.

Yellow Rattle at Bloody Oaks, June

Right: Musk Mallow (white form) and Bladder Campion at Horn Mill, July.

Left: Common Mallow, Tixover, June.

Meadowsweet and Meadow Cranesbill, South Luffenham, August.

Right: Clustered Bellflower at Ingthorpe, August.

Text by Graham Worrall, Botany Recorder, Rutland Natural History Society. Photographs by Graham Worrall, George Sellars, Irvine Cushing

A Year of Rutland's Fungi

Over 300 different species were identified in Rutland over four years by Rutland Natural History Society members. Mushrooms and toadstools are fruiting bodies which disperse spores – some drop from gills or pores – some are shot from tiny flasks. Many only erupt at a certain season, others emerge when it is warm and wet throughout the year. Hard rusty brackets may last for years, delicate fungi only a few days. Some recycle dead material; a few attack the living, but most live with trees which provide nourishment, and they in turn feed the trees. All the while, under the ground or within tree trunks, are hidden mats of root-like threads, gathering to send forth the fungi we see.

Morel *(Mitrophora semilibera)* **occurs in damp verges and woodlands.**

Spring

Velvet Shank *(Flammunlina velutipes).* **'Little flame with velvet feet'. Withstands frosts well.**

Winter

Earth Star *(Geastrum triplex).* **Spores puff away from the ball.**

Below: Bracket *(Ganoderma adspersum).* **Spreads spores which look like cocoa.**

Above: Sulphur Tuft *(Hypholoma fasciculare).* **Forms dense clusters on stumps.**

Left: Stink Horn *(Phallus impudicus).* **The sickly smell from the tiny cap attracts flies which carry off the spores.**

Summer

Larch Bolete *(Suillus grevillii)* **is only found with Larch trees.**

Right: Oyster Mushroom *(Pleurotus ostreatus)* **is delicious to eat.**

Text by Linda Worrall, Mycology Recorder, Rutland Natural History Society. Photographs by Patrick Mann and Irvine Cushing

ENVIRONMENT

Rutland's Lichens

Rutland has a rich lichen flora, on tree bark, rock quarries, soil and stonework. Several hundred species have been recorded since the 1970's. Lichens are unusual plants in being symbiotic – an association of a fungus with an alga. They are extremely slow growing but often very long-lived; some local specimens are probably several hundred years old. They are eaten by a variety of insects and invertebrate animals. They are especially valuable to man in indicating old, undisturbed habitats such as ancient woodland. Lichenologists can even date habitats by listing the lichens found there.

To most of us, lichens give colour and interest to the countryside and no walker should be without a small handlens for inspecting these fascinating plants.

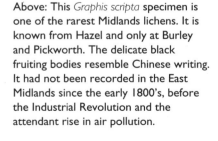

Above: Old coppice Hazel is extremely valuable in ancient woodland. The oldest boughs bear lichens previously thought extinct in the Midlands. These species are often extremely small and inconspicuous. The finger points to a small specimen of *Graphis scripta.*

Above: This *Graphis scripta* specimen is one of the rarest Midlands lichens. It is known from Hazel and only at Burley and Pickworth. The delicate black fruiting bodies resemble Chinese writing. It had not been recorded in the East Midlands since the early 1800's, before the Industrial Revolution and the attendant rise in air pollution.

Left: *Thelotrema lepadinum* is another extreme rarity, known from only two places in the Midlands. It was thought extinct since the 1830's until this relic population was found at Burley on Hazel. *Thelotrema* species are especially common in the Tropics. The fruiting bodies look like volcanoes under a x10 handlens.

Ancient Woodland

Until the late 1980's Midland woodlands were thought to be lichen deserts. However, the discoveries at Burley Wood in 1989, have shown that they are valuable refuges for many lichens once thought to be extinct.
Even the acidic bark of Oak (shown here), especially where sheltered and bordering sunny rides, bears numerous species. These trees are very vulnerable however, and their lichens can disappear when exposed to wind-borne drift of agricultural fertilizers from nearby fields. More than 200 lichens have been recorded at Burley Wood since 1989; it is now a Site of Special Scientific Interest and has been assessed as the best ancient woodland for lichens in the midlands by the British Lichen Society.

Churchyards

Natural rock outcrops do not occur in Rutland. However, the county abounds in rocky substrata provided by man. Old churchyards are especially valuable, being densely covered with lichen species. A single local churchyard may contain 70 species. The church walls can be even richer.

Left: The crustose lichen *Lecanactis abietina* occurs only in ancient woodland in the Midlands. It is abundant in crevices on shaded bark of Oak at Burley Wood, Clipsham and Pickworth. To some observers it imparts a curious mauve fluorescence to tree trunks when exposed to sunlight.

Left: The foliose lichen *Parmelia saxatilis* prefers the uppermost branches of acidic bark of Oak in Rutland. The lobes are covered in tiny particles called isidia which, carried on the legs of insects, help the lichen to colonise new sites. Lichens like these were once used for dyeing wool.

Pertusaria pertusa is another crustose lichen of the bark of old trees. However, it is not confined to old woodland and can be found on old Ash in hedgerows sheltered from the south-westerly winds which carry polluted air.

Left: Sheltered Elder and Sloe, especially beside ponds and swamps, bear pretty orange and grey species on their twigs. Many of the lichens of Elder also grow on concrete and limestone because of their calcium content. Shown here are orange *Xanthoria parietina* and grey *Physcia adscendens,* amongst Sloe berries at Pickworth.

Left: Limestone tombs bear many orange lichens which prefer sunny faces. Here is *Xanthoria calcicola.* This particular leafy species grows very rapidly for a lichen, by about 7mm per year! Crustose lichens on the other hand, grow by a mere 1-2mm per year. It is possible then, by measuring its diameter, to calculate how old a lichen is.

Above: A scarce lichen in Rutland is *Xanthoria elegans.* It is found on bird perches on natural rocks around the Arctic. But in Rutland, it grows only on flat concrete tombs and parapets, provided they are perched on by birds. Many lichen species seem to need bird-lime as a source of nutrients.

Right: *Lecanora subcircinata* was one of the first lichens ever to be recorded in the Midlands – in 1795 from the Vale of Belvoir. It is fairly common on limestone in churchyards and especially on canal and railway parapets. Like many lichens, it likes sunshine.

Wayside Trees

Wayside Ash, in hedgerows, carries an abundant lichen flora in Rutland, especially in shelter. This example has *Parmelia sulcata* and *Evernia prunastri*. Old Willows are also good habitats for lichens. Wayside trees can be especially interesting when they are being colonised by crustose lichens, so they are worth looking out for.

Evernia prunastri was once considered nearly extinct. It is intolerant of sulphur dioxide air pollution. However, since the early 1980's it has made a spectacular comeback on wayside trees, especially Ash and Willow, even in the centre of Oakham. This is because sulphur dioxide pollution has markedly decreased due to Clean Air Acts, and the reduction in domestic and industrial coal burning. Not all lichens are coming back though, and many continue to decline because of increasing toxic nitrogen compounds in the atmosphere, arising from farm animals, motor exhausts, etc., and from chemicals in agricultural fertilizers and acid rain.

Even woodwork can bear a lichen flora. Here is *Physcia caesia* on a wooden fence. Many lichen species also colonise asphalt, asbestos and roof tiles on houses, even ironwork and old boot leather.

Rocks and Soil

Although natural rock outcrops do not occur, Rutland has many man-made outcrops in the form of quarries and gullets. Rock faces, screes and soil can bear lichens.

Right: The soil lichens in gullets, such as at Market Overton are similar to those of heathland. *Cladonia* species are especially frequent, such as this one – *Cladonia floerkeana*. The red tips are fruiting bodies, producing fungus spores for dispersal.

Left: *Peltigera,* the dog lichens – *Peltigera rufescens* is shown here, live on grassy soil in gullets and sometimes on old gravel paths. Dog lichen is named after its one-time medicinal use as an antidote to hydrophobia, after being bitten by a rabid dog. Whether the remedy worked is not recorded.

Text and pictures by Dr Anthony Fletcher Leicestershire Museums, Arts & Records Service

Oakham Gargoyles

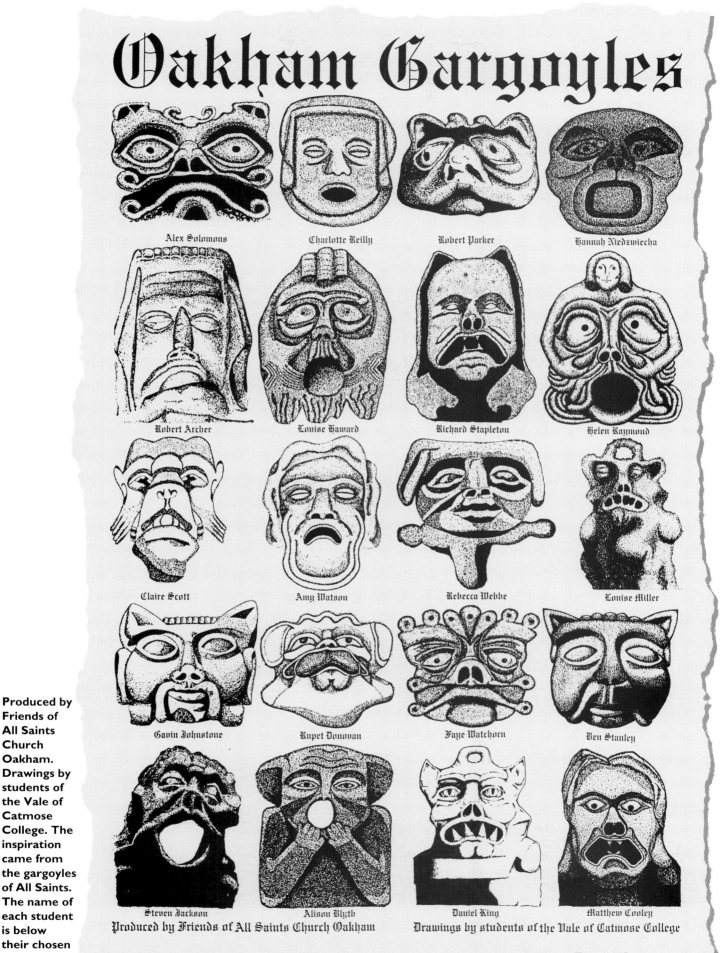

Alex Solomons   Charlotte Reilly   Robert Parker   Hannah Niedzwiecha

Robert Archer   Louise Haward   Richard Stapleton   Helen Raymond

Claire Scott   Amy Watson   Rebecca Webbe   Louise Miller

Gavin Johnstone   Rupet Donovan   Faye Watchorn   Ben Stanley

Steven Jackson   Alison Blyth   Daniel King   Matthew Cooley

Produced by Friends of All Saints Church Oakham   Drawings by students of the Vale of Catmose College

Produced by Friends of All Saints Church Oakham. Drawings by students of the Vale of Catmose College. The inspiration came from the gargoyles of All Saints. The name of each student is below their chosen gargoyle.

25

Old Picture Postcards
of Rutland

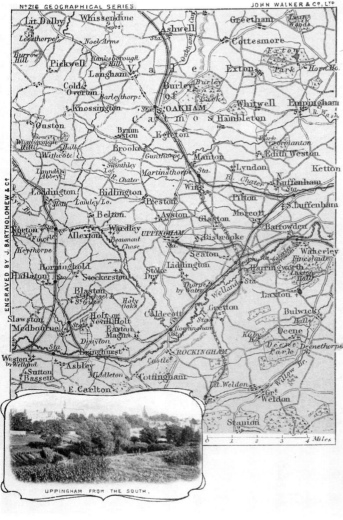

Andrew Jenkins

Map of Rutland. Circa 1904. Published by John Walker & Co. Ltd. A turn of the century map postcard depicting the western side of the county. Note the extensive network of railways then serving the area, most of which have now been closed. The course of the Oakham Canal can be seen at the top of the map. The most prominent features on a modern map of this area are, of course, the Eye Brook Reservoir and Rutland Water.

Old picture postcards provide a unique record of Rutland as it was during the first 25 years or so of the 20th century. They were used as a means of communication much as we use the telephone today and because of their popularity many millions were printed. Collecting both new and used picture postcards became fashionable with the result that many have survived and they are now being re-collected. One such collector is Andrew Jenkins whose book *Rutland – A Portrait in Old Picture Postcards* was published in 1993. Throughout *A Celebration of Rutland* you will find old picture postcards of Rutland loosely collected together under various headings, and many of them are reproduced for the first time. Andrew gave free access to his collection and many of his postcards are included. The remainder were provided by Dr Trevor Bell, Bryan Waites, David Griffiths, June Lawton and Robert Ovens. Andrew also provided many of the notes accompanying the postcards, and prepared the historical introduction which follows.

Collecting Old Picture Postcards

One hundred years ago, on the 1st of September 1894, a Post Office regulation was altered permitting the use of privately published illustrated postcards as well as the plain official postcards previously available.

This change in the rules was the birth of the picture postcard. It entered the world in an era of great social change. The Industrial Revolution was at its height and the rapid communications provided by the railways allowed people to travel long distances to find work, whilst for many, holidays and tourism were a new found luxury.

People soon realised that the new picture postcards fulfilled a need for rapid pictorial communication at a time when newspaper illustrations were poor and the radio and television were yet to be invented. It was possible to send a picture of your town or village to distant friends and relatives. The postcard arrived at its destination within twenty four hours of posting or even on the same day all for the price of a ½d stamp. As the latest techniques of photography and colour printing were used the cards made very attractive souvenirs.

It is hardly surprising therefore, that postcard sending became extremely popular and at the turn of the century a craze developed for collecting postcards with the album a prized possession in many an Edwardian drawing room. At the height of the postcard mania in 1907 over two million cards were sent everyday in Britain. Local photographers and publishers sprang up to cater for the demand, illustrating every possible scene and event.

Rutland was no exception with over twenty publishers operating in the county at the turn of the century.

These early postcards are recognised as important historical documents as they record in great detail life in Edwardian Britain. The correspondence on the back of the card can provide an added bonus as it often gives a personal touch to the picture on the front. For example, on a card of Uppingham School Cadet Corps on parade before leaving for France in 1915, the sender, a pupil at the School, has written "The school is rather empty this term and we are taught only two days per week". Thus this postcard has turned into a piece of living history.

After 1910 the introduction of the cinema and telephone led to a decline in postcard sending with a brief respite during World War I. For many years after, postcard collections lay neglected in cupboards and attics. Recently however, they have been rediscovered and are now very collectable.

All's Well at Oakham. Circa 1908. Unknown publisher. An embossed and gilded greetings postcard typical of the Edwardian era.

Andrew Jenkins

Early Postcard Publishers

Bell's Series – Market Overton
Billow's Series – Melton Road, Oakham
P.W. Bowman – Oakham
K.S. Bristow – Langham
J Burton & Sons – Oakham
S. Cooke – Hambleton
Dolby Bros. – Uppingham
Drake & Son – Uppingham
H. Ellingworth – MeltonRoad, Oakham
W.E. Exton – Oakham
Halliday Series – Oakham
J. Hawthorne – Uppingham
H.P. Holt – High Street, Oakham
Chas. Matkin – High Street, Oakham
K.S. Roberts – Oakham
E.D. Smith – Market Place, Oakham
W.J.W. Stocks – Uppingham

Text by Robert Ovens and Andrew Jenkins

HISTORY

Oakham Castle

In the centre of Oakham, approached by a lane from the Market Place, stands the Great Hall of Oakham Castle. Before the Norman Conquest, the castle and its manor belonged to Edith, widow of Edward the Confessor. After her death, the church and part of the manor passed to the Abbey of Westminster, while William the Conqueror took the castle into his hands. We learn from Domesday Book that in 1086 he had a hall here, and this was probably associated with a motte and bailey castle which once stood at the south-east corner of the site.

This first hall, most likely a wooden building, was replaced in about 1180-90 by the magnificent stone hall which we see today. Built by Walkelin de Ferrers, a Norman baron, it is generally recognised as one of the finest late 12th century domestic buildings in England.

The remains of other structures lie beneath the grass of the inner bailey which surrounds it. Together they would have formed a fortified manor house, rather than a castle in the usual sense. The whole was defended by earthen banks and stone walls, with at least two towers. To the north, in Cutts Close, there were gardens and fishponds.

Inside the hall there is a splendid range of Romanesque figure sculpture. Above the capital of each of its six fine columns there is a musician, each playing a different instrument. Though damaged, they are of superb quality. Other sculptures can be found around the building; outside, the gable ends are surmounted by two finial sculptures, of a centaur and of Samson and the lion. Almost certainly, the stonework was carved by masons who had worked at Canterbury Cathedral, using local stone from Clipsham.

The castle was the residence of the lord of the manor of Oakham. Sometimes, the king held the manor himself and visited the castle. We know that the other buildings included a chapel, a gaol, stables and barns. By the early 16th century many of these buildings were ruinous. However, the Great Hall continued in use as a courtroom, the hub of both the manor of Oakham and the county of Rutland.

Indeed, a new courtroom was added in the 18th century, and the main entrance to the hall was probably moved to its present central position at about the same time. Assize courts were held here until 1970.

Today, Magistrates' Courts are held weekly, and occasional Crown Courts and Coroner's Inquests still take place. The castle is looked after by Leicestershire County Council's Museums, Arts and Records Service, and is open to the public - it has probably been visited by the curious for several hundred years.

Above: Two of the many horseshoes in Oakham Castle, showing the coronets of a marquis and earl. Far left: General view of the east wall of Oakham Castle.

Horseshoe Custom

● The castle is also renowned for the unique spectacle of more than 200 great horseshoes which hang on its walls. These represent the ancient custom that every peer of the realm, on his first visit to Oakham, must forfeit a horseshoe to the lord of the manor.

● The custom has been followed for at least 500 years; the earliest known reference to the deposition of a horseshoe is to one from Edward IV in about 1470. A large elaborately wrought horseshoe headed by a plain shield matches the description of his horseshoe, and this is perhaps the earliest to survive.

● However, it is very likely that the custom has its origins in the late 11th century, soon after the Norman conquest, and should be regarded as a Norman joke, a play on words. The Ferrers family, to whom the castle was granted, came from Ferrières in Normandy and were ironmasters. The word 'farrier' comes from the same source, and the French for a horseshoe is 'fer à cheval'

● The custom is still valid, though there has not been a presentation since 1981, when Lord Lane, then Lord Chief Justice, surrendered his forfeit to Joss Hanbury, Lord of the Manor. Are there others waiting in the wings?

The long line of the law. Although court cases have been heard at Oakham Castle for hundreds of years it is only recently that the lists of offenders have taken on such mammoth proportions, like this 42 foot computerised catalogue of cases leading to the door of the 12th century building.

Text by Tim Clough, Keeper of the Rutland County Museum

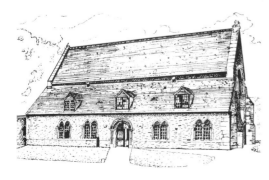

Oakham Castle drawn by Sarah Morris, a student at the Vale of Catmose College.

Rutland County Museum

I t was in 1794/95 that Sir Gerard Noel Edwards erected the warm ironstone building which houses the Rutland County Museum just outside the centre of Oakham in Uppingham Road.

Sir Gerard, who lived just over the road at Catmose (now the Council offices) was Colonel of the Rutland Fencible Cavalry. This was one of the many small regiments raised to serve as local defence forces at the time of the French Revolution. The purpose of the large building was an indoor riding school for the regiment.

The museum is now home to a rich collection of items of rural life, illustrating the historic past of Rutland. Military origins are reflected in a special gallery devoted to the history of the Volunteer Soldier in Leicestershire and Rutland.

Right: The interior of the Rutland County Museum showing the unusual roof structure of the Riding School of the Rutland Fencibles.

Village Life

In the riding school, which is remarkable for its wide, double pitch roof built of Baltic timber, the displays illustrate the archaeology of Rutland; its rural trades and occupations; domestic life and agriculture.

There are comprehensive collections of tools and equipment of the tradesmen on whom village life depended – the wheelwright and carpenter, the blacksmith and farrier, the cooper, cobbler and tinsmith, plumber and decorator. The veterinary care of livestock is covered and there is a delightful simulation of a farm kitchen at the turn of the century, with fittings from local buildings.

In the Poultry Hall, built by Rutland Agricultural Society in the mid-19th century, there is more emphasis on aspects of farming life such as dairying, crop production and the barn. A rare 1917 Saunderson tractor was acquired by the Friends with Science Museum grant aid.

A courtyard links the buildings and here, as elsewhere, many objects on open display are accessible to visually or physically handicapped visitors.

Friends

● The museum has grown considerably since it was opened by Princess Alice, Duchess of Gloucester, in 1969. The princess accepted invitations from the Friends of the Museum to return for its tenth and twentieth anniversaries.

● The Friends have twice provided funds to purchase additional buildings which were part of the original complex. They have also supported the development of the extra premises – first the stable block which now provides a meeting room, the Volunteer Soldier display and reserve collection space; and, more recently, Number 2, Catmos Street, adjacent to the main museum. To coincide with the bicentenary of the Riding School, this is being converted into the Colonel Noel Suite, providing self-contained meeting and refreshment facilities as well as additional displays. This work has been aided by a grant from the Museums and Galleries Commission.

● The Friends have also purchased numerous items for the museum's permanent collections.

Agricultural displays in the Poultry Hall.

Text by Tim Clough, Keeper of Rutland County Museum. Photographs Leicestershire Museums, Arts and Records Service.

Research

Visiting students and members of the public make frequent use of the museum's extensive collection of historic photographs of people and places in Rutland. People travel from far and wide to carry out family history research with the aid of the museum's library and supporting material. Many of them join the Rutland Local History and Record Society which is based at the museum.

There is a well equipped meeting/teaching room, extensively used by visiting schools. Leicestershire Museums' teaching service draws extensively on the collections and on documentary sources to enable children and their teachers to get the best out of their museum visits. Much of the material in the displays and in the reserve collections is directly relevant to national curriculum teaching and GCSE project work.

Part of the Leicestershire County Council Museums, Arts and Records Service, Rutland County Museum sets out to give visitors an impression of life in Rutland over the past 200 years. By combining the collections of Oakham School (mainly archaeological) with rural life material brought together by the late Mr E.G. Bolton at Casterton Secondary School, and by adding to these over the years, the museum now has a collection of more than local importance. It is one of which Rutlanders can be justifiably proud.

Rutland Documents
& the Record Office

Work of the Record Office

Leicestershire Record Office is part of Leicestershire County Council's Museums, Arts & Record Service. It is the centre of manuscripts, books, maps and photographs of Leicestershire and Rutland. Based in a converted Victorian school with purpose-built storage, the Record Office offers state-of-the-art conditions for some five shelf-miles of collections and an attractive range of facilities for researchers. Rutland archives in the Record Office's care cover a broad spectrum, from records of courts and local authorities to those of churches, businesses, schools and landed estates. Access is free by reader's ticket (obtainable at the Record Office on production of formal identifying documents).

Above: The Record Office's searchrooms can accommodate up to 44 researchers at any one time. The most heavily used sources, including parish registers and census returns, are available on self-service microfiche or microfilm.

The Record Office's strongrooms are constructed to meet the stringent environmental and security requirements of the British Standard on storage and exhibition of archival documents (BS 5454). Mobile shelving makes the most of every square metre of floor space.

The Record Office's experienced conservation staff are fully occupied repairing documents damaged by the ravages of time and hard usage.

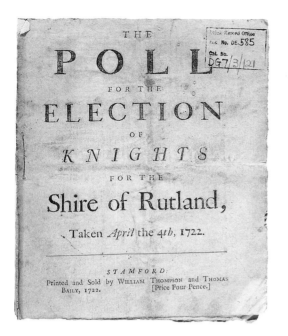

Reference Number DG7/3/121

Pages from a poll book published after the Rutland election of 1722. It lists the voters in each parish and shows how they voted. Under the unreformed franchise the vote in county elections depended on ownership of freehold property worth 40 shilling per annum and voters were often not residents of the parishes where their property and vote lay. In this election Daniel, Lord Finch and Sir Thomas Mackworth were successful. Lord Finch, the eldest son of the Earl of Nottingham, had been elected first in 1710, at the age of 21.

Right: This curious map, not really a map at all more a fanciful sketch, was drawn by William Hole to illustrate Michael Drayton's poem, 'Poly-Olbion, or a Choragraphicall Description of all the Tracts, Rivers, Mountaines, Forests and other parts... of Great Britain'. The Rutland 'map' appears only in the second edition of 1622.

Reference Number 9D49/42

Reference Number
DE2876/2

❝

Small shire that can'st produce
To thy proportion good
One vale of special name,
One forest and one flood.
Oh Catmos, thou fair vale,
Come on in grass and corn,
That Belvoir ne'er be said
Thy sisterhood to scorn.

❞

Extract from Poly Olbion (1612) by Michael Drayton.

AN ACCOUNT OF THE Population of the County of Rutland, TAKEN IN THE SPRING, 1795.

Names of Parishes.	Men	Women	Boys	Girls	Total.
Ashwell,	56	53	31	33	173
Ayson,	35	38	11	10	94
Braunston,	106	109	87	71	373
Burley,	64	60	55	46	225
Bisbrooke,	57	62	55	38	212
Brooke,	21	32	28	18	99
Barrow,	22	22	23	43	110
Barrowden,	120	143	112	113	488
Belton,	80	86	114	135	415
Cottesmore,	61	70	116	119	366
Casterton Great,	83	84	58	42	267
Casterton Little, with Tolthorpe,	28	31	28	30	117
Clipsham,	47	58	40	23	168
Caldecott,	73	96	80	64	313
Egleton,	27	28	36	53	144
Empingham,	208	217	147	133	705
Edith-Weston,	78	96	47	38	259
Essendine,	36	35	22	20	113
Exton,	208	218	122	130	678
Glayston,	52	52	23	36	163
Gunthorpe,	2	2	2	3	9
Greetham,	86	91	97	111	385
Hambleton,	53	62	99	121	335
Ketton, with Geeson,	209	218	118	119	664
Langham,	128	158	87	82	455
Luffenham North,	73	86	75	76	310
Luffenham South,	62	68	46	31	207
Liddington,	159	165	130	114	568
Leighfields,	6	7	17	16	46
Lyndon,	25	33	22	9	89
Manton,	51	64	52	39	206
Morcott,	96	106	67	70	339
Martinsthorpe,	1	1	1	1	4
Market Overton,	113	120	76	86	395
Normanton,	19	14	3	1	37
Oakham Lord's-Hold,	319	381	236	207	1143
Oakham Dean's-Hold, with Barleythorpe,	91	106	149	128	474
	36	28	21	12	97
	72	92	57	53	274
	13	21	11	8	53
	48	52	43	36	179
rpe,	136	141	91	79	447
	55	57	27	33	172
	88	112	71	59	330
	15	19	17	11	62
	42	54	21	15	132
	34	33	12	16	94
	22	24	32	30	108
	48	63	49	42	202
	39	47	26	20	132
	14	14	13	13	54
	381	462	303	209	1355
	73	82	46	43	244
	19	25	15	11	70
	132	156	116	126	530
	16	19	9	6	50
Total,	4238	4772	3492	3231	15733

Above: The first national census took place in 1801. However, interest in population growth, and particularly its relationship to poverty and the poor rates, had been growing for some time. Such concerns may lie behind this census of the Rutland parishes, taken in the spring of 1795, which records not only total figures but breaks them down further into male and female adults and children. The original document was found pasted inside the cover of the Morcott parish register.

The Exton Manuscripts

The family papers of the Noels, Earls of Gainsborough, were deposited in the Leicestershire Record Office in 1987. The collection was the largest single deposit of family archives ever received by the Leicestershire Records Office. With the help of grants from the Pilgrim Trust and the Leverhulme Trust an archivist has been employed specifically to catalogue the collection. The Exton manuscripts span the period from the twelfth to the twentieth century and have proved an exciting and important addition to the Leicestershire Record Office's existing holdings on Rutland.

Reference Number DE3214/157/6

Thomas Blore published the first and only part of his *History and Antiquities of Rutland* in 1811. It was dedicated to Gerard Noel Noel of Exton Park who had let Blore have the run of the family muniments for his research. While some of Blore's papers subsequently found their way into the British Library, the whereabouts of the bulk of his notes for the unpublished portion of his *History of Rutland* was, until recently, a mystery. Blore's notes were found in the Exton MSS. and this transcript of medieval deeds relating to Exton, was presumably prepared for publication.

Right: Colonel Gerard Noel Noel, who succeeded to the estates of his uncle Henry, Earl of Gainsborough in 1798, was interested in agricultural improvement, an early supporter of the short-lived Leicestershire and Rutland Agricultural Society and a prominent member of the Rutland Agricultural Society founded in 1830. This poster gives the premiums for a show of stock to be held at Exton in October 1811. The reason for the postponement of the ploughing match until March, was that Colonel Noel had gout.

Reference Number DE3214/351/2

George Moore Henton was born in Leicester, the son of a senior clerk at Paget's Bank, in 1861. He trained as an artist and on his death in 1924, in addition to his paintings, left a large collection of photographs. These found their way to the Museum in Leicester and are now in the care of the Leicestershire Record Office.

The collection consists of nearly 2000 images. Henton's range of subjects was immense, from street scenes and social events to architectural studies and informal portraits. Leicestershire and Rutland views figure prominently, often including the group of children which is almost a 'trademark'. Most of the photographs were taken during the last years of the nineteenth century and the first decades of the twentieth. Henton was meticulous in recording exactly where and when each one was taken.

The Henton Collection

The 'weir' or pond at Barrowden with the Marquis of Exeter's Arms (Edwin Wootton, publican and blacksmith) in the background. Monday 21st August 1916, 1.37 pm.

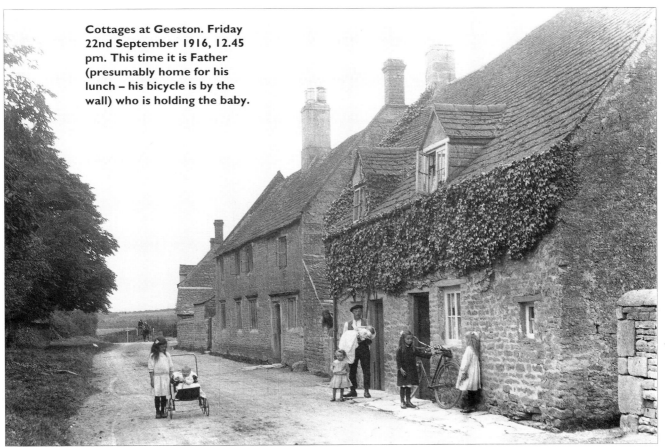

Cottages at Geeston. Friday 22nd September 1916, 12.45 pm. This time it is Father (presumably home for his lunch – his bicycle is by the wall) who is holding the baby.

Above: All Saints,
Braunston 1830s.
Right: All Saints,
Braunston 1790s.

The great wave of Victorian restoration changed the appearance of many churches. What did our churches look like before this restoration? A collection of 67 drawings in the Fine Art Department, Leicester Museum, shows Rutland churches in the 1790s. An album of drawings and watercolours owned by Uppingham School Archives shows all Rutland churches in the 1830s. The former was described in an article in Rutland Record No. 9, 1989, and the latter in the book *Rutland Churches Before Restoration*, edited by Gillian Dickinson, 1983. Examples for the Oakham Benefice are illustrated here.

HISTORY

Rutland's Historic

> " *No region in England can show so many fine churches in such a small area.* "
>
> **W G Hoskins**

Above: St Peter,
Brooke 1830s.
Left: St Peter,
Brooke 1790s.

Top: **St Andrew, Hambleton 1830s.**
Above: **St Andrew, Hambleton 1790s**
by Nathan Fielding.

Above: **All Saints**
Oakham 1790s. Note
single gable over
chancel and north aisle
which existed until
1857. Right: All Saints
Oakham 1830s.

Churches

Above: **St Edmund,**
Egleton 1830s.
Left: **St Edmund,**
Egleton 1790s.

The Cost of Conservation

Roof Leadworks

£7,200

All Saints Oakham

All Saints, and many churches like it all over the land, is not only a famous landmark but also an intrinsic part of our heritage. We should miss it if it vanished and yet it is a constant struggle to maintain and repair our churches. Here you see only a few of the jobs being done and the cost, which will secure the church for the future.

The programme of work shown in these illustrations, plus many more fabric repairs, would not have been possible without generous help from benefactors, grants from the Rutland Historic Churches Fund, Leicestershire County Council and Oakham Town Council as well as the support of the Insurers in meeting the claims for malicious and accidental damage.

Clock Face Repairs

£1,670

Repairs to Cock Peter and the Spire

£6,050

Cock Peter by John Barber

Once more I'm on my lofty perch,
  All glistening, fresh and hale,
Once more atop the Parish Church
  I guard the Catmose Vale.

As now I see the summer close,
  Watch homeward coming sheaves,
I'll mourn the autumn fading rose,
  I'll mourn the falling leaves.

With autumn done and winter near,
  I'll wait the swirling snow,
But still aloft with never a fear
  I'll guard the town below.

With winter gone, new life around
  I'll greet the burgeoning spring,
And listen for the cuckoo's sound;
  I'll greet the birds that sing.

But through the seasons as I stand,
  There's one thing I abhor:
The Cottesmore planes so close at hand,
  The cursed Tornado's roar.

Boiler House flooding Repairs

£2,500

Left: Back to terra firma, thanks to steeplejacks Rob Hurley and John Peart with the Vicar, Canon Charles Mayhew.

Rutland Times

Schedule of Fabric Maintenance and Repair August 1992

Repairs to stonework	£5,000
Plain leaded light windows	£10,000
Roof leadwork	£15,000
Pew platforms	£15,000
Wire screens to stained glass	£6,500
Floor covering to aisles	£9,000
Totals (net) excluding VAT and architects fees and contingencies	**£60,500**

● Note this is a rolling programme and there is not a direct comparison with all figures shown near illustrations

Replacement of Pew Platform

£3,900

Photographs and part of the text by K W Weatherhogg

Rutland Churches

Ketton   Hayley Wildman

Burley   Chris Coleman

Ryhall   Richard Holt

MARKET OVERTON   Market Overton   Annabel Wattan

Egleton   Merry Smith

Normanton   John Walker

Brooke   Jamie Maddison

Braunston   Nicola Gray

Clipsham   Michael George

Whissendine   Duncan Miller

Tixover   Gary Perkins

Emma Clark

Sold in aid of The Rutland Historic Churches Preservation Trust

Drawings by Pupils of the Vale of Catmose College, Oakham.

Drawings by students of the Vale of Catmose College, Oakham. Sold as a tea-cloth for the Rutland Historic Churches Preservation Fund.

40

Rutland Bats

With a wingspan of around 15 inches, noctule bats feed high over tree tops, often well before dark.

Noctule by R E Stebbings

■ RUTLAND BATS

Eight of Britain's 14 species of bats have been recorded in Rutland in recent times. The commonest is the tiny pipistrelle which, with the long-eared bat, is found in most of our towns and villages. The other species are found infrequently, with Barbastelle and Leisler's being the rarest, each discovered once in the last 20 years. Species such as Natterer's, Whiskered and Daubenton's bats rely mostly on buildings, while noctule bats usually use hollow trees. Parts of Rutland seem well suited to bats and we have several, good-sized colonies.

Where bats have been found

- ■ Pipistrelle
- ■ Brown Long-eared
- ▲ Whiskered
- ▲ Natterer's
- ● Daubenton's
- ● Noctule
- ▼ Barbastelle
- ▼ Leisler's

The rapid twisting flight of the pipistrelle is a common sight at dusk.

Right: Appropriate advice can prevent bats being killed by toxic chemicals. Below: Bats like this brown long-eared use echo-location to find moths in the tree-tops.

The way they live

Bats are the only mammals that fly, and our British bats eat insects. Although the males are solitary for most of the year, the females live in complex social groups. In summer they give birth to a single baby which must be able to fend for itself within five or six weeks. Bats survive our cold winters by hibernating, perhaps for as long as six months, when they are very vulnerable to cold weather and disturbance. They are long-lived creatures, relying on traditional maternity and hibernation roosts and it is thought the locations of these sites is learnt by the young from their mothers. Their amazingly sophisticated echo-location enables them to catch insects and find their roosts in total darkness.

Brown Long-eared Bat by R E Stebbings

Helping Bats

Bats are harmless to man, and may even be beneficial as a biological pest control. They deserve our tolerance and respect.

● Bats can be helped by providing access to roofs, with holes at gable apexes or under eaves and soffits. They need be no larger than 20mm wide.

● Planting flowers, shrubs and trees which attract insects, especially night-scented flowers, will provide much-needed food.

● Remember to consult English Nature for advice before you do anything which might affect them or their roosts.

Pipistrelle by S. Dalton / NHPA

The threats

With their low birth rate and vulnerable way of life, bat numbers have declined by up to 75% in the last 20 years. This has resulted in full protection being given to bats and to the places they roost. What are the threats they face?

● Exclusion from summer roosts through building repairs and barn conversions.

● Hibernation roosts lost or disturbed.

● Scarcity of food, and loss of feeding areas, such as hedgerows and woodlands.

● Intolerance, resulting in exclusion from roosts.

● Bad weather makes insects scarce and in spring prolongs hibernation beyond what their fat reserves can cope with.

● Timber treatment still kills hundreds of bats and their babies.

Timber spraying by M Boulton / ICCE

Habitats

Burley Wood / Rutland Water by J Harris

Burley Wood and Rutland Water support rarer bats – noctules and Daubenton's.

Egleton Meadow by J Harris

Insects abound in old hedges and hay meadows, even on windy nights.

R E Stebbings

Modern houses are warm and dry, providing many nooks and crannies for bats to roost.

M Frankum

Some Rutland churches shelter as many as three different types of bats. Cool and undisturbed, they are ideal for hibernation.

Text by Jenny Harris, Bat Recorder, Rutland Natural History Society

Below: Holly Blue: Numbers
fluctuate from year to year.
In Spring, eggs are laid on
holly and in Summer on ivy.
Often breeds in towns.

**Right:
Elephant
Hawk Moth.
Often seen on
honeysuckle at
dusk. Trunk-
like snout of
caterpillar
gives the
insect its
name.**

**Right: Buff-tip.
A moth
named for its
buff wing-tips.
Resembles
small length of
broken branch
as camouflage.
Present near
Rutland
Water.**

**Lesser Swallow Prominent
Moth. This female has just
laid eggs on the leaf.
Known to be present on
Egleton Nature Reserve
and in Prior's Coppice.**

**Brimstone. One of the
easiest species to identify.
It can be seen in most
months of the year. The
caterpillars feed on
buckthorn.**

ENVIRONMENT

Moths & Butterflies

Below: Small Tortoiseshell. One of the first on the wing after hibernation. Can be found anywhere in Rutland feeding from flowers.

Below: Small Copper. Variation in the size of black marks occurs on the copper colour. They frequent grassland and old quarries.

Left: Gatekeeper. A butterfly of hedgerows and woodland rides is seen here on Fleabane. They live in well defined colonies.

Far left: The Magpie Moth. A pest of gooseberries and currants with striking wing patterns. Numbers have declined in recent years.

Orange Tip. Visits Garlic Mustard or Cuckoo Flowers in woods such as Prior's Coppice. Look for them in April and May.

Lime Hawk-Moth. Can be found in the towns of Rutland. A slow flier that does not feed in the adult stage of its life cycle.

Text by Jean Harvey. Photographs by Ray Butchart and R.H. Harvey.

Jean and Ron – RH – Harvey are Entomological Recorders for Rutland Natural History Society.

around the county

Excavations...

Since the Roman occupation limestone, clay and ironstone have been invaluable resources in the county. Both Ketton and Clipsham stone have been widely used in the construction of many fine buildings, restoration work and sculpture. Only five operational quarries now remain in Rutland and other uses include the manufacture of hand-made bricks and cement for the building industry, and the limestone is crushed and used for agricultural purposes.

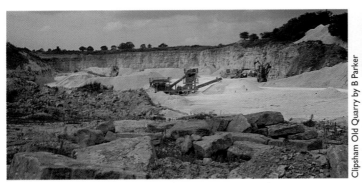

Clipsham Old Quarry by B Parker

Above: Deserted quarries leave large holes flanked with waste material but wildlife quickly adapts. Plants re-establish themselves and thickets of thorn and bramble grow on the soil and disintegrated shale.

Right: As a quarry matures, trees and shrubs soften the landscape, providing protection and valuable habitat for insects, birds and animals.

Adders, Grass Snakes and Slow-worms inhabit quarries where they bask in the sun but always remain alert and ready to retreat if disturbed. Left: This Grass snake was found in the Leicestershire & Rutland Trust for Nature Conservation reserve at Bloody Oaks quarry.

Photograph by G H Sellars

Photograph by G H Sellars

Lime-loving plants, the Common Spotted orchids can be found growing in grassy areas in many of Rutland's quarries during June and July.

Photograph by R H Butchart

Left: The Marbled White butterfly is distinguished from other native brown and white species by its black and white chequered markings.

Below: Green Woodpecker *(Picus viridis).* Graphic by Michael Iannantuoni. Taken from part of an original painting by Hilary Burn.

Text by Barbara Parker, Recorder, Clipsham Quarry Survey Group, Rutland Natural History Society

Clipsham Old Quarry by G H Sellars

to wildlife havens

Left: Green Hairstreak butterflies take full advantage of the warmth and shelter of quarries. Extremely territorial, they lay their eggs in May and June on a wide range of plants, from low-growing herbs to shrubs.

Right: The Slow-worm is known as a legless lizard and attains an average length of 30cm.

Photograph by R H Butchart

Photograph by G H Sellars

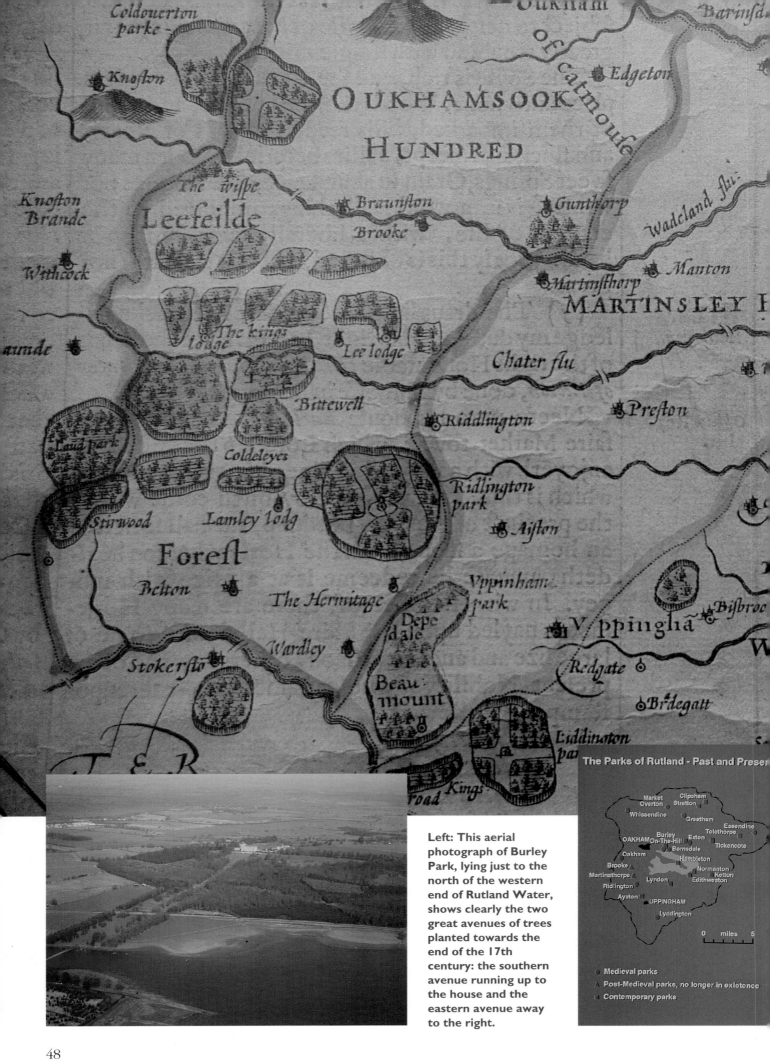

Left: This aerial photograph of Burley Park, lying just to the north of the western end of Rutland Water, shows clearly the two great avenues of trees planted towards the end of the 17th century: the southern avenue running up to the house and the eastern avenue away to the right.

The Parks of Rutland - Past and Present

• Medieval parks
▲ Post-Medieval parks, no longer in existence
■ Contemporary parks

Exton Park today shows the familiar late 18th century landscape associated with Capability Brown.

ENVIRONMENT

Parks of Rutland

There have been parks of various kinds in Rutland, as in every other county in England, for more than 900 years. The first parks were introduced by the Normans, mainly to cater for their love of hunting, and were stocked with deer for this purpose.

They were usually wooded areas, to provide covert for the deer, and were securely enclosed, normally by an earth bank, topped by a wooden paling fence, with an inside ditch.

There were at least ten such hunting parks in the county in the Middle Ages at Barnsdale, Burley, Essendine, Exton, Lyddington, Market Overton, Oakham, Ridlington, Stretton, and Whissendine and traces of some of them can still be found in the landscape in the form of earth banks, hedges and field names.

By the end of the fifteenth century, these parks began to change in character and, over the next two hundred years, in place of hunting parks 'amenity' parks came into existence.

Still largely wooded and surrrounded by wooden paling fences, as maps of the period show, they were designed to provide an appropriate setting for the new and often grandiose houses that were being built. Rutland examples are the now ruined early 17th century Exton Hall, and Tolethorpe Hall, rebuilt about the same time.

From about 1600 onwards another change took place with the coming of the era of formal landscaped parks, based on designs brought over from France. Among their main features were formal gardens around the house, lakes, and avenues of trees. A good example of the latter is still to be found in Burley park.

Towards the end of the seventeenth century, there were at least four parks in Rutland: at Burley, Exton, Brooke and Martinsthorpe, though only the first two have survived.

The next major development occurred in the second half of the 18th century with the introduction of the familiar landscape style, particularly associated with Capability Brown. Major features were sweeping lawns with the grass coming right up to the house, groups of trees, lakes, and summer houses, as can still be seen at Exton today.

The 19th century witnessed the laying out of more parks around new or rebuilt country houses, as at Ayston, Clipsham, Edith Weston, Ketton, and Tickencote. In the later 1800s, municipal parks appeared, the first parks to be opened to the general public. Presumably because it has no towns of any size, Rutland has no municipal parks, the nearest approximation being Cutt's Close in Oakham.

Rutland Farm Park

In recent years parks have been changed and developed in various ways. One example is Rutland Farm Park, originally the private park attached to Catmose House, at the southern end of Oakham

Above: Ridlington Park still existed almost 400 years later, as can be seen from this extract from John Speed's map of Rutland of 1611. Other parks shown are at Lyddington, Uppingham, Oakham (right against the county boundary, next to Cold Overton Park in Leicestershire). The well-wooded nature of Leighfield Forest also shows up clearly.

Text by Leonard Cantor

Botanical Painting

Although botanical illustrations are very popular at present, especially for interior design work, they have a long and distinguished history.

Perhaps the most famous artist in this medium was Redouté (1759-1840), known as the Raphael of Flowers and considered one of the greatest botanical illustrators of all time.

Botany and natural history had long been a serious study for country gentlemen, particularly the rural clergy. Gilbert White's *Natural History of Selborne* (1781) was compiled in the spirit of this movement. So was his brother-in-law, Thomas Barker's observation of weather and nature. As Squire of Lyndon Hall in Rutland, Thomas kept meticulous records throughout the 18th century. However, so far, few of his sketches have been discovered.

At Market Overton, Rutland, Anne-Marie Evans carries on the great tradition of botanical painting. Her garden has matured to give her an abundance of flowers from which both she and her students find inspiration.

Some twenty years ago she realised that students of all ages and abilities are able to become competent botanical painters if taught the right way. She has developed a method detailed in *An Approach to Botanical Painting* (1993) co-authored with her husband Donn Evans, which displays her own great enthusiasm and skill.

Anne-Marie, living in out-of-the-way Rutland, has become an international figure. She is a regular visiting tutor at the New York Botanical Gardens where she conducts Master Classes several times a year.

Recently, she launched the UK's first certificated Botanical Illustration course at London's historic Chelsea Physic Garden. She founded, and is President of the Leicestershire Society of Botanical Illustrators and runs courses at her home each summer, both for beginners and advanced students.

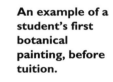

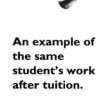

An example of a student's first botanical painting, before tuition.

An example of the same student's work after tuition.

Photographs Ann-Marie Evans

A corner of the garden at the Old Manor House, Market Overton.

I'm often asked, "Why is your garden called Barnsdale when you live a good mile away just outside Exton?" When I first came to Rutland in 1977, I rented a small cottage from the redoubtable Mrs.Dickenson at Barnsdale Hall. It attracted me because it had a couple of acres of good land with it, tailor-made for my purpose.

I was editor of *Practical Gardening* magazine at the time and I needed somewhere to grow plants for photographs and to conduct gardening trials for the magazine. This place was perfect.

Luck seemed to follow me around at that time because after a couple of years, the garden caught the eye of the series producer of the BBC's TV gardening programme *Gardeners' World*. Unknown to me, he was looking for a replacement for Arthur Billet's famous garden at Clack's Farm because Arthur was retiring. Well, to cut a long story short, I got the job and, fingers crossed, I'm still here!

But by 1983, the garden had become too small and Mrs. D had decided in any case, to sell. I needed somewhere else and fast. Once again, my luck held.

A small stone farmhouse up the road came on the market and, joy of joys, it had five and a half beautiful acres with it. It was just a square, flat field, but it had a good barn, plenty of storage space and the field hadn't been ploughed in living memory. That meant that, though the soil was heavy, it was full of fibre and easy to cultivate – just what the doctor ordered.

ENVIRONMENT

Barnsdale
with Geoff Hamilton

Within days I was making dozens of journeys with my small trailer up and down Exton Avenue transferring all my precious plants. And I took one other important thing with me.

Because viewers had only just got used to my first garden, it was felt that a change of name would be confusing and unsettling. So, I took the name with me too and Barnsdale Mark II was born.

It was all done in a bit of a rush because we record the programme only the week before it's transmitted, so the first one from the new garden was all about how to move gardens!

In feverish haste I managed to cobble together a reasonable garden for the first few weeks while I concentrated on turning my five acres into a series of gardens made for television.

Now there are a dozen small gardens, each different, where we can demonstrate ideas and techniques and Barnsdale has become the most "visited" garden in the country.

We record a large part of the programme here every week during the spring and summer with only one, big problem. The noise of aeroplanes drives us to despair!

With RAF Cottesmore just up the road, we can more or less guarantee an ear-splitting Tornado jet overhead every five minutes or so. We have to record our peaceful little gardening programme in between. Mind you,the Air Force do their best. We tell them in advance when we're recording and they do try to limit the noise on those days. So they tell me!

My producer spends the first half hour of his visit every week, wandering round looking for what he calls 'cock-ups'. I can get away with very little. The seeds that don't come up, the plants that die for no reason at all, the weedy patches we've not had time to get around to, they all go in. Fortunately,they represent a very small percentage of what I think I can claim as overall success.

Courtyard in 1984.

Courtyard in 1992.

Geoff Hamilton at the Drought Garden on Barnsdale car park at Rutland Water.

Strangely, the one main complaint I receive is about my soil."Well,it's all right for Hamilton" they say, "just look at his lovely soil."

Well, the fact is that, though my soil is basically good, it also gets about 100 tons of manure every year and it's treated with a great deal of respect.Like all gardeners, I have to work at it.

I'm fortunate to have a wonderful team of colleagues to help. Because of the popularity of the garden on television, we receive hundreds of requests to visit personally. Alas, this is something we just can't contemplate. The programme is seen by anything up to five million people so we would expect to attract literally thousands of visitors. However careful they were, that number of feet would create havoc. So, in order to provide *Gardeners' World* viewers with a taste of Barnsdale, we are now in the process of laying out another five and a half acres next door.

Barnsdale Plants and Gardens is open every day and will eventually be an even better garden than the original and made especially for the public to enjoy. The nursery sells rare and unusual garden plants, mainly propagated from the television gardens and we're getting on well with laying out the gardens.

To provide ideas for smaller plots, we're establishing a whole series of small gardens. There's the *Daily Express* cottage garden we built for the *Gardeners' World Live Show* in 1992, a *Radio Times* garden from the same show, a pool and bog garden, an alpine feature, an Elizabethan kitchen garden, a herb garden that featured on *Gardeners' World* and a small town garden.

Next on the list is a knot garden made in very formal design with low box hedging and an 'artisans cottage garden' to be used in a new TV series.

It's a busy, happy life and hopefully, we can make our contribution to the enjoyment of other gardeners and introduce many more to a fulfilling and absorbing pursuit.

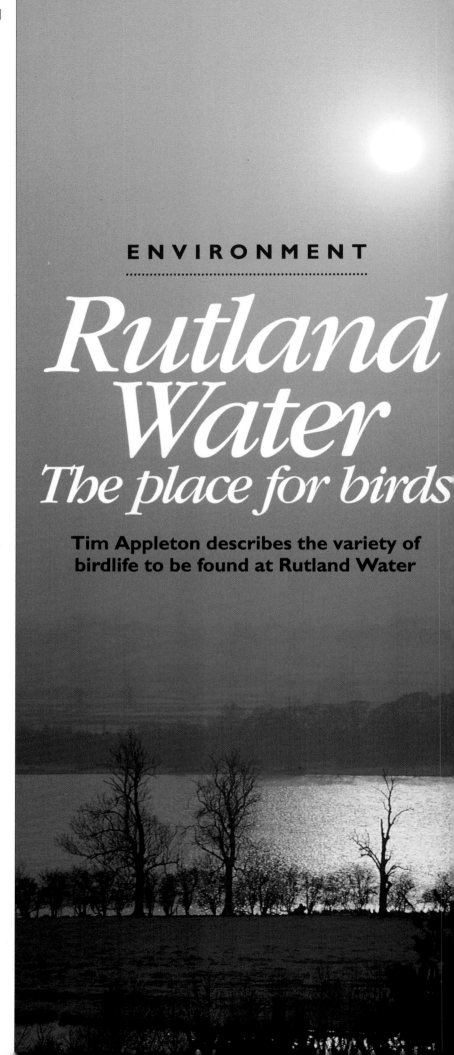

ENVIRONMENT

Rutland Water
The place for birds

Tim Appleton describes the variety of birdlife to be found at Rutland Water

Gordon Langsbury

Above: If you want to see Gadwall – head for the hides at the Egleton Nature Reserve

Rutland Water is beautiful in all seasons. Here a wintry sun sets over the lake.

C M Debney

Birds come to Rutland Water for many different reasons. Some make a brief stop to rest and feed whilst on migration, others over-wlnter and some spend the summer rearing young. This diverse use of the reservoir means that there is always a wide range of birds to be seen.

The huge expanse of water attracts all types of water birds which find the convoluting shorelines, reedbeds, wader scrapes, deep and shallow waters ideal for their lifestyles. Woodlands such as Hambleton and Barnsdale complement the new plantations and provide homes for a very different group of birds.

Aerial feeders find rich pickings in the summer months when millions of insects emerge from the water.

For the waterfowl enthusiast the winter months provide a wealth of wildfowl when thousands of birds displaced from the colder climate of Europe arrive.

Wigeon are the most numerous and their numbers often exceed 4,000. They will be seen grazing the short grass swards near the car parks and pastures grazed by sheep during the summer months.

Out in the deep water ducks such as Tufted duck and Goldeneye dive in search of invertebrates on the floor of the reservoir. In recent years Cormorants escaping the rough seas of coastal Britain have taken to spending the winter months at Rutland Water. A few of these large black birds have even stayed to breed.

Occasionally, rare winter visitors find their way to the reservoir and these may include Black or Red-throated Divers, Slavonian or Red-necked Grebes.

Sea ducks also stray inland and

Scaup, Scoter and Long-tailed Ducks are frequently seen.

Spring is heralded by the early arrival of Sand Martins and Wheatears in March – both are migrants that arrive here after an exhausting journey from Africa.

As the weather improves many more migrants can be seen either over the water, singing in the woodlands or from the reed-lined margins of the reservoir. Blackcaps, Willow Warblers and Nightingales, to name but a few, are found in the woods, while Reed and Sedge Warblers, Reed Buntings, and Yellow Wagtails are seen close the the water's edge.

As summer progresses broods of ducklings, goslings and cygnets dart across the waters stabbing at hatching insects. At least twelve species of waterfowl have been recorded breeding, including the rarer ones such as Garganey, Teal, Shoveler and Pochard. In recent years Kingfishers and Grey Herons have begun nesting, the latter for the first time in Rutland since 1830.

Perhaps one of the most familiar sights and sounds of the summer comes from the Common Tern colonies that nest on artificial islands at the nature reserve. These beautiful birds grace the waters from mid-April until early September.

Spotted Redshank, Little Stint and Ruff are some of the strange names given to a group of birds known collectively as waders. Up to nineteen species of waders have been recorded at Rutland Water in a single autumn day as they probe into the exposed muddy shoreline in search of food.

By late August thousands of ducks and geese have gathered at Rutland Water to moult. Unlike other bird species, wildfowl cannot fly during this period and as the water offers safety, food and resting sites the reserve has become a major British moulting site.

Among the teeming flocks of ducks can be found one particular species, the Gadwall, which occurs at Rutland Water in numbers far greater than any other site in Britain.

Although the wildfowl are in their dull plumage during the autumn, birdwatching visitors can be assured that Rutland Water offers some of the best birdwatching facllities anywhere in Britain – remember some of the avian visitors have travelled up to 6,000 miles to visit us — a sure sign that Rutland Water is the place for birds.

Text by Tim Appleton, Warden at Rutland Water Nature Reserve

> *One of the finest examples of creative conservation in Great Britain*

Sir David Attenborough

Rutland Water is one of the largest reservoirs in Britain. It received Royal Assent in 1970 and was opened in 1976. It was intended to supply water to the expanding towns and cities around. Since it was in the lowlands and accessible to large populations it has had a major role in providing recreational activities for the area. Because of this widespread use it is necessary to reconcile the conflicting demands of walkers, cyclists, environmentalists, farmers, tourists, fishermen, sailors and others who comprise the thousands visiting Rutland Water each year.

Above: Oakham with Rutland Water beyond.

Recreational Fact File

- Nature Reserve: Birdwatching Centre Egleton; Lyndon Visitor Centre
- Trout Fishing – one of the finest in Europe
- Sailing and Windsurfing – Rutland Sailing Club and Day Sailing
- Walking and Nature Trails
- Cycling from Whitwell and Normanton
- Rutland Belle pleasure cruiser
- Barnsdale Drought Garden and Arboretum
- Normanton Church Museum
- Adventure Playgrounds
- Butterfly and Aquatic Centre
- Restaurants at Whitwell and Normanton

Birdwatching, Sailing, Cycling and Relaxation

Below: View towards the Nature Reserve at sunset.

Nature Reserve

● Rutland Water Nature Reserve was born in April 1975 when the Leicestershire and Rutland Trust for Nature Conservation joined forces with Anglian Water Authority. The Trust was given the opportunity to develop and create a wildlife sanctuary on a scale never before achieved in Britain. The area chosen for the Nature Reserve were the two arms of the western end of the water. Once flooded, this area consisting of extensive shallows, irregular shorelines and undisturbed lagoons, would provide the wildfowl with ideal conditions for feeding, breeding and roosting.

● A Warden was appointed to oversee the creation of the new habitats, the construction of birdwatching hides and to organise a voluntary wardening scheme. Initially the bulk of the work was the planting of more than 40,000 trees and shrubs, all from local stock.

● Throughout the winter months, each weekend saw different organisations from the local community planting willows, ash, oak, and alders, to create shelter belts, plantations, hedgerows and screening. The success of many wildlife reserves lies in providng a diversity of habitats and a reed bed was planted using the roots collected from Burley Fishponds which were later flooded as the water levels increased.

● Seventeen years later the fruits of those pioneering labours have resulted in the maturing of the habitats which in turn has attracted more than 240 different species of birds. Rutland Water has received national and international acclaim as a wildfowl sanctuary. Both the EC and the World Wide Ramsar Convention have recognised its importance and the site has now been notified a Special Protection Area and a Ramsar site.

Text by Tim Appleton. Photography Richard Adams and David Moore

Trout Fisherman magazine

The one that didn't get away – a delighted fisherman at Rutland Water.

HISTORY

Keeping Time in Rutland

Knowing the time instantly and accurately is a recent luxury brought about by modern technology. Before mass produced low-priced clocks and watches were imported from America in the second half of the 19th century, relatively few people could afford them. Up to this period in Rutland, where the main occupation was farming, there was little need for accurate timekeeping as dawn, dusk, the seasons and other natural phenomena, such as the positions of the sun and the stars in the sky, controlled people's lives. In any case, agricultural wages were very low and the majority of the workforce couldn't consider owning a clock even if they were able to find a use for one.

What is believed to be the first timepiece recorded in Rutland, and now in the Rutland County Museum, is a water clock found at Market Overton during the excavation of a Saxon cemetery. It is simply a bronze dish with a hole in its base and when placed on the surface of water it takes about an hour to gradually fill and sink.

The Saxons used sundials and one found in 1929 during site excavations was placed on the east wall of the Ram Jam Inn. In medieval times, crude versions of these dials were scratched onto the south facing wall of many churches and these are known as 'scratch dials'. A hole in the wall held a stick or a piece of metal which created the shadow. Most of the original dials had three or four lines radiating from this hole to indicate important times in the day. It is thought that the primary function of the scratch dial was to denote the time of prayers and a bell would have been rung to call people to worship. The church services in many Rutland villages would have been regulated by scratch dials in this way before a church clock was installed.

This bronze dish found at Market Overton is believed to be a Saxon water clock.
Leicestershire Museums, Art Galleries and Records Service

When visiting one of Rutland's fine churches it would be an interesting and worthwhile exercise to see if it still possesses a scratch dial; don't be surprised if you find one somewhere other than on the south facing wall! A warning here, don't confuse scratch dials with bench marks.

Scratch dials won't be found on every church, but this is not at all surprising as many fabric alterations have been carried out over the centuries. Quite often scratch dials were carefully preserved during such work, but there are cases where the stones with the dial on were replaced upside down, incorporated in a new wall on the north side of the church, or covered by a new porch.

Burley on the Hill (SS/RO)

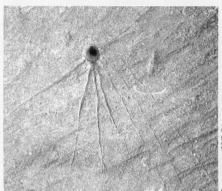

Braunston (SS/RO)

Manton (SS/RO)

Stoke Dry (SS/RO)

These scratch dials can be seen on the Rutland churches of Burley on the Hill, Braunston, Manton and Stoke Dry. Can you find them?

Text and compilation by Sheila Sleath and Robert Ovens

Bell Ringing

● The Saxon sundial and the later scratch dial were obviously ineffective on sunless days. During the medieval period and much later, the hour glass, water clock and candle marker were also employed to record the passage of time. However the majority of Rutlanders would really have had no need of such devices; the pattern of their daily lives was so attuned to Mother Nature that they possessed a sense of time which was quite sufficient for their needs. Even so the ringing of a church bell would for many centuries have played an important role in communicating time within Rutland communities. An early reference to bell ringing can be found on one of the Norman pillars supporting the chancel arch in Stoke Dry Church.

● Some churches had a sanctus bell which was originally rung during services so that all the villagers could join in the holy song of adoration. Later it was rung to indicate the start of services and the bell was often hung in a small bellcote on the gable end of the chancel roof. Two such bellcotes can be seen on Manton and Market Overton Churches.

A stone carving of a bell ringer in Stoke Dry Church.

● A 5am 'morning bell' and an 8pm 'curfew bell' were rung in many villages from the time of the Norman Conquest right up until the 20th century. 'Curfew' is from the French 'couvrefeu' meaning 'cover the fire'. It was originally introduced as a fire prevention measure and for a long time it was the signal for all taverns and ale houses to close. Later on it was rung to guide travellers on dark winter nights. In South Luffenham, 'Bell-ringing Close' was donated to the church by a woman who was saved by the 'curfew bell' after she had been lost on Luffenham Heath. The income from the field was used to pay the sexton for ringing the bell each evening from September until March, and this continued until 1914.

● The 'gleaning bell' was rung daily during harvest time in at least twenty Rutland villages until the start of the First World War. A few villages continued this as a tradition well into the 1920s. Gleaning was the collection of the remaining corn in the fields after all the 'stooks' had been gathered in. In Ketton for example, it was rung at 9am and 5pm and marked the start and end of gleaning which was carried out by the women and older children of the village.

● Edith Sleath, a lifelong resident of Belton in Rutland remembers her grandmother, Elizabeth Marlow, who was born in 1859, talking about the church bell being rung to inform the workers in the fields that it was 'dinner-time'. There is more detail on this in *Leicestershire and Rutland Notes and Queries* 1889-91. The Rev. Newmarch writes that the 'one-o'clock' bell "has been rung from time immemorial. The payment for it is included in the sexton's salary, it being part of his duty". He also added that some of his older parishioners remembered "a bell rung at 5am Summer and Winter..... We have also had, until within the last 20 years or so, a 'pancake bell' rung at noon on Shrove Tuesday."

Sundial on the porch at Ayston Church. Photograph taken at 1.30pm G.M.T.

Right: The sundial at St.Peter's Church, Belton in Rutland. Photograph taken at 10am G.M.T.

Left: The numerals on this sundial at Wardley Church have almost disappeared due to weathering. It was originally dated 1694.

Sundial on the porch at Preston Church. Photograph taken at 10.30am G.M.T.

Scientific Sundials

It was during the 16th and 17th centuries that scientifically constructed sundials came into use and these were often located on churches, usually above a south facing porch, but sometimes on the tower. They not only indicated the time to the local population, but also provided a means of regulating the church clock. However, because of the earth's elliptical orbit round the sun, scientific sundials only show the correct time on four days of the year. For the rest of the year they are either 'fast' or 'slow' compared to an accurate clock. The maximum 'errors' are sixteen minutes fast in November and fourteen minutes slow in February.

Although a number of these church sundials have survived, only a few can still indicate the time. Good examples of 'working' sundials can be found on the church porches at Ayston, Belton, Preston and Caldecott. Many others in Rutland, like that at St. Botolph's Church, Wardley, are now virtually unreadable.

A series of mid 18th century water colours and drawings of Rutland churches in the Uppingham School Archives,

Sundial on the front of 'The Crown' in Uppingham.

Above: A modern sundial on the porch at Caldecott Church. Note the inscription. Photograph taken at 12 noon G.M.T.

Right: Braunston Church in 1839, showing the sundial on the south wall.

Below left: 'Sundial House', Uppingham.

show a number of sundials which have now disappeared. One example is at All Saints' Church, Braunston, where there used to be a large sundial on the south wall.

Another water colour shows a very interesting sundial on the tower of Market Overton Church, said to have been the gift of Sir Isaac Newton (1642 -1727) whose grandmother lived in the village. It was quite unusual as there were two dials at right-angles to each other on the south-west corner of the tower. All that now remains is one of the gnomons – all traces of the dial markings have weathered away. (The gnomon, which is Greek for "one who knows", is that part of the sundial which produces the shadow).

By the middle of the 16th century it had become common practice to include these "proper" sundials as architectural features on the facades of large houses, stables and public buildings. Although many of these have disappeared we know where some of them were by reference to books and old documents. For example, James Wright's *The History and Antiquities of the County of Rutland* published in 1684 has engravings of buildings with sundials, including Martinsthorpe House, Exton Hall and Luffenham House.

Travelling around Rutland one can spot sundials in many locations. In Oakham, for example, there is a 'Tempus Fugit' sundial on the front of a building in High Street. In Uppingham there is a sundial on the front of 'The Crown' in High Street East and further down the street, away from the market place, is 'Sundial House', complete of course, with a sundial.

'Tempus Fugit' sundial in High Street, Oakham.

'Sundial House' Morcott.

Turret Clocks

The first church clocks were made in the 13th century but they probably didn't reach Rutland for another two hundred years. They had a verge and foliot escapement and were not very accurate, hence the need for regular checking against a sundial.

One of the earliest church clocks in Rutland, which would be of this type, was at Ridlington, where it is reported that "in 1618 the clock and chimes were out of repair and would not go". Later on, in 1681, the churchwardens were ordered by the Archdeacon to "amend the dial in the churchyard" – was this a reference to a sundial or the clock dial? There is no longer a clock at this church and there is no record of when it was removed. There was another early clock in Exton Church, as in 1618 "it was presented that the church clock did not go right, but made a great rumbling when it did go." A drawing of 1839 shows a clock dial on the east face of the tower, but in 1843 a massive bolt of lightning struck the spire and the subsequent fire destroyed much of the church.

The first church clocks in Rutland didn't have dials – a bell struck by the clock mechanism communicated the time – and the works would normally have been located at the foot of the tower. Although some were later converted, the majority were eventually replaced by pendulum clocks with two handed dials. The introduction of the dial meant that the works had to be located higher in the tower so that the dial could be seen from afar. The problems and costs of creating a clock chamber and finding a suitable location for the dial meant that some of the earlier works were not replaced when they became unreliable. This has probably resulted in there being fewer Rutland churches with clocks now than there were three hundred years ago. The 'Rutland bellcote' presented particular problems as there wasn't a tower for the works or dial.

The pendulum was invented by Galileo about 1640 and further developed in Holland by Christian Huygens. Robert Hooke invented the anchor escapement a few years later. These developments, within a period of less than twenty years, resulted in a dramatic improvement of timekeeping accuracy.

This technology, developed mainly for more accurate time-keeping in domestic clocks was also applied to church and other turret clocks. The old 'Commonwealth' clock from St. Mary's Church, Edith Weston, which is believed to have been made by John Watts of Stamford in 1658, was converted in 1775 by Richard Hackett of Harringworth to include a pendulum, the more accurate anchor escapement and a single handed dial. When a new clock was installed in 1928 the old one was removed and retained in the church. It remained there almost forgotten until 1966 when it was fully restored. The clock is now in the Rutland County Museum where it is on display as a working exhibit.

The bellcote on St. Nicholas' Church, Pilton.

Braunston Church from the Brooke road.

Below: The clock at St. Peter and St. Paul's Church in Wing, installed in 1920, is dedicated to soldiers who lost their lives in the First World War. There must have been an earlier clock in this church as the Archdeacon's Visitation of 1605 noted that it "was taken away by the widow of Mr. Cooke, the late parson".

SS/RO

Left: The old clock on display in Clipsham Church.

Below: Normanton Park Hotel clock.

The old church clocks of Empingham and Clipsham were almost certainly made by John Watts as both are marked with 'IW' (Iohannes Watts) and the date. The Empingham clock, now in the Stamford Museum, was replaced by a new clock when the church was restored in 1859. The clock John Watts installed in St. Mary's Church Clipsham has also been removed and restored and this now stands on display in the church. It is dated 1688. The cost of these clocks when new was about £10 each, including installation.

There is some evidence to show that another of Watts' clocks was installed in the tower at All Saints' Church, Tinwell. Although there's no trace of the works now, records show that "they were wanting a clock" as early as 1619. The current clock was installed in 1929. It is often stated that many of these old church clocks were made by local blacksmiths, but whilst they had the skills to make some of the components, an understanding of the mechanism and the manufacture of the gear wheels and pinions would have been a problem to many. What is probably closer to the truth is that these early turret clockmakers started out as blacksmiths and then specialised.

Whilst all later clocks carry the maker's name, most early clocks were anonymous and undated – John Watts was a rare exception – although occasionally the details are given in churchwardens' accounts. In the clock chamber of St. John the Evangelist's Church at Caldecott there is a panel on the wall which may give the name and date of the clockmaker – George Woodcock, 1724. The old clock at St. Mary's, Morcott, was replaced in 1921. The clock bell, which was inscribed 'ad moneo cum moveo' ('While on the swing I warnings bring') was almost certainly made by Richard Holdfeld of Cambridge between 1599 and 1612, thus indicating the date of the original clock. It hung above the parapet on the south west corner of the tower. The bell is shown in a drawing of 1839, and was still there in 1880 according to Thomas North in *The Church Bells of Rutland*. It is now kept inside the church. We have a clue as to when the clock was installed at St. Andrew's, Glaston, as the corbels which support the dial are dated 1739. A small clock bell used to hang outside the south light of the spire, but it has now been removed.

The clock at Holy Cross Church, Burley on the Hill, was made by the eminent London maker Joseph Knibb, who was clockmaker to Charles II. It is one of only two turret clocks made by him, and the top part of the iron frame bears the inscription 'Joseph Knibb London 1678'.

Oakham All Saints' Church clock was made in 1858 by Frederick Dent. He was the stepson of Edward Dent, who, in 1852, started the manufacture of The Great Clock of the Palace of Westminster, commonly referred to as 'Big Ben'. Edward died in 1853 and Frederick completed the clock in 1855, but it wasn't installed until 1859. Both this and the Oakham clock strike the 'Westminster Chimes' which originated from Great St. Mary's Clock in Cambridge. They are more correctly called the 'Cambridge Chimes'.

Most of the clocks now working in Rutland churches were installed during the 19th and early 20th century. Some of these were commissioned to commemorate significant events, such as the Coronation of Queen Victoria, or in memory of local people.

The clock at St. Peter's, Belton was given by two sisters in memory of their brother, Robert White Baines who died in 1887. This must have been a replacement clock because a water colour of the church shows that there was a clock dial there in 1839. At the turn of the century a clock was installed in Braunston Church by Mr. Hanbury, a local farmer. The dial was placed above the tower parapets so that his workers could see it from the Brooke road.

The large houses built by the aristocracy in Rutland from the beginning of the 17th century had attached stables, and a clock over the entrance to the stable yard became a decorative as well as a functional feature. Unfortunately a number of these houses and their stables have been demolished. However, 17th century Lyndon Hall remains complete with its clock in the tower above the entrance to the stable yard. Although Normanton Hall itself was demolished, its stables were retained along with the stable clock. These stables are now Normanton Park Hotel.

Dial styles

Another interesting exercise is to compare the different types and styles of clock dial on Rutland churches and other buildings. Look at the shape (round, square, diamond, hexagonal or octagonal), the style (flat, convex or skeleton; gilded or painted numerals; the shape of the hands) and the material it is made from (timber, cast iron, stone or slate). Can you see anything which gives a clue to the age of the dial or the works behind it? If you are able to go inside the building you might find a dedication plaque, and in some churches the historical notes give details of the clock. You may even find an old clock on display. You will need special permission however to visit the clock chamber, as they are usually locked and access is often difficult.

Left: The cast iron skeleton dial on the church of St. Mary in South Luffenham. Note the use of a convenient window to connect the dial to the works.

Right: Painted timber dial on All Saints' Church, Tinwell. It is probably a replica of John Watts' original dial.

Left: Stone dial on St. Mary's Church, Edith Weston. Notice that the space between the numerals is divided into four confirming that there used to be a single handed clock here.

Right: St. Andrew's, Glaston. The painted timber dial sits on corbels dated 1739.

Domestic Clocks

The earliest domestic clocks were made on the Continent but by 1658, following the work by Galileo, Huygens and Hooke, weight and spring driven pendulum clocks were being made in England. They almost immediately took the now well known form of the longcase (grandfather) clock and the bracket clock.

The first domestic clockmakers in England were trained on the Continent and worked mainly in London. Clockmaking however, quickly spread to the provinces although it was concentrated mainly in the larger towns. Case styles continued to be influenced by the London makers, but by 1750 provincial clockmakers had developed their own designs. Country longcase clocks became smaller and less elegant, and many had square brass dials with 30 hour movements which had to be wound every day.

At this point it is probably worth relating the unfortunate experience of a certain Mr. Mears who thought he had a 30 hour clock:

'There was a man who had a clock
His name was Mr. Mears.
And every night he wound that clock
For five and forty years.
And when at last that clock turned out
An eight day clock to be,
A madder man than Mr. Mears,
I never hope to see.'

From *Stamford Clocks & Watches* by Laurence Tebbutt.

The first recorded Rutland clockmaker was Blackburn (we don't know his Christian name) who was working in Oakham between 1720 and 1750. A number of his clocks have survived and one is in the Rutland County Museum. The only other early Rutland clockmaker recorded is John Wilkins who was working in Oakham in 1740.

By the early 19th century clockmaking in Rutland had virtually ceased owing to factory production methods and cheap imports. This meant that there was a large increase in clock ownership and as a result local clockmakers concentrated on repair work and turned to selling clocks which were 'bought in', often adding their own names to the dials.

During the 18th century Stamford was an important horological centre and at least ten clockmakers are recorded as working there during this time. No doubt much of the demand for domestic clocks in Rutland, such as it was, was met by these Stamford craftsmen, but some will have been supplied by Leicester, Melton, Grantham, Market Harborough and Oundle makers, especially as demand grew towards the end of the century.

It is known that by 1771 Richard Hackett had set up a clock factory just outside the county in Harringworth employing a large number of people. Very few of his clocks are known today and it is fairly definite that he supplied movements and dials to other clockmakers who put their own name and town on the dial. However, he engraved an 'H' on his clocks and many of these have been noted. Richard Hackett died in 1782 and the site of his factory is now a farm.

By 1780 painted dials were being introduced and an excellent example is the longcase clock made by Stephen Simpson for the Oakham Union Workhouse, now the Catmose Vale Hospital. He had a shop in Market Place Oakham and the clock was commissioned by the Guardians of the workhouse in 1837. It is exhibited in the Rutland County Museum and has paintings of the Common Seal of Rutland in each corner of the dial and the workhouse in the dial arch.

Blackburn's clock in the Rutland County Museum. Unusually, all known examples of his clocks have serial numbered dials. This one is 1058 and it is thought that he probably started numbering at 1000. The highest known serial number is 1208.

The dial of Stephen Simpson's Oakham Union Workhouse clock.

Leicestershire Museums, Art Galleries and Records Service

Leicestershire Museums, Art Galleries and Records Service

Watchmaking

Very little is known of watchmaking in Rutland although many craftsmen advertised as watchmakers as well as clockmakers. Those that were made in the county would have been special commissions for wealthy customers. One Rutland watch which has survived, now in the Newarke Houses Museum in Leicester, is a silver cased pocket watch made by J. Simpson of Oakham. It is numbered 5045 and the London hallmark on the case has the date letter for 1795.

Leicestershire Museums, Art Galleries and Records Service

J. Simpson's silver cased pocket watch.

The tracing, recording and preservation of Rutland's horological heritage is of paramount importance because "Time waits for no man". Fortunately museums display clocks from the past under good environmental conditions and their longevity is assured. By and large, antique domestic clocks in private hands, because of their increasing value, are cherished. Church clocks are also well maintained, and this is thankfully more to do with church heritage and tradition than their market value. A few of our Rutland sundials have been expertly restored as a result of the refurbishment of a commercial building, but most of the rest are in various states of disrepair. Many of our scratch dials have virtually disappeared due to weathering. Fortunately most of those remaining have now been identified and recorded for posterity.

In 20th century life digital clocks and watches, the Speaking Clock, radio and television ensure that everyone has instant and affordable access to very accurate time information. The old scratch dials, sundials and clocks of Rutland are part of our heritage, and we should not forget that throughout the ages they played a significant part in ordering the lives of the 'Raddlemen'.

Old clocks and their makers

The following table lists all the known Rutland clockmakers up to 1870 and readers may find this useful in dating their own antique clocks. Note that dates given refer to a particular year or period when it is definitely known that a clockmaker was working. There may also be other clockmakers whose work has not yet been recorded.

Name	Premises	When working
William Aris	Horn Lane, Uppingham	1798 to 1835
Thomas Aris	High Street Uppingham	1835 to 1876
John Bates	Market Place, Uppingham	1846
Blackburn	Oakham	1720 to 1750
Stephen Blackburn	Oakham	1770
Thomas Cooke	High Street, Oakham	1828 to 1849
John Cooke	High Street, Oakham	1864 to 1876
Mark Flint	High Street, Uppingham	1864
J. Fox	Uppingham	1775
Joseph Furniss	Uppingham	1785 to 1795
Richard Hackett	Harringworth (Northants)	1754 to 1771
John Houghton	High Street, Uppingham	1828 to 1849
Edward Hubbard	Oakham	1770 to 1780
John Jackson	Melton Road, Oakham	1846
Stephen Rodley	Market Place, Oakham	1863
J. Simpson	Oakham	1795
Stephen Simpson	Market Place, Oakham	1828 to 1855
James Sparkes	Market Place, Uppingham	1855 to 1864
John Wilkins	Oakham	1740

More details about local clocks and clockmakers are given in the following:

■ *The Making of Clocks in Leicestershire and Rutland* by John Daniell (1951).
■ *Leicestershire Clockmakers* by John Daniell (1975).
■ *Stamford Clocks and Watches* by Laurence Tebbutt (1975).
■ *Leicestershire and Rutland Clockmakers* by Patrick Hewitt (1992).
■ *Turret Clocks in Leicestershire and Rutland* by Patrick Hewitt (1994).

All known watchmakers and clockmakers are listed in:

■ *Watchmakers and Clockmakers of the World* Vol.1 by G.H.Baillie.
■ *Watchmakers and Clockmakers of the World* Vol.2 by Brian Loomes.

For more general information on country clocks:

■ *Country Clocks and their London Origins* by Brian Loomes (1976).
■ *White Dial Clocks* by Brian Loomes (1974).

All the above should be available through local libraries, but some may be for reference only. There are also many books dedicated to clocks and clockmakers in other areas, as well as more general titles covering styles and mechanisms, and these are useful for dating purposes. Knowing the clockmakers name, where he was working and when, will enable the reader to carry out more research in parish registers, directories and other documents at appropriate County Record Offices. Examples of local clockmaking can be seen in the Rutland County Museum, the Newarke Houses Museum in Leicester, and the Stamford Museum.

There are some 196 bells in the County of Rutland. Thirty-one of these are said to have been cast before the year 1600 and many of them are still as originally cast, that is they have survived the centuries without cracking therefore having to be melted down and recast.

Over the years several churches have added to the number of bells they have. This has continued to the present day and will no doubt continue to do so. Some 29 bells have been added to towers in the county in this century.

No evidence has ever been found of a bell foundry existing in the county, though in 1876 some fused bell metal was found in the churchyard at Empingham. This is thought to have been left over as a result of casting bells in the churchyard – probably for Empingham Church itself.

The nearest bell foundry to Rutland was that of Tobie (Tobias) Norris of Stamford. His earliest bell for Rutland was the 2nd at Little Casterton in 1606, and his last was the 3rd at Ayston in 1626. He is buried in the north aisle of St. George's Church, Stamford.

Other bell foundries which supplied bells to Rutland were located in Loughborough, Peterborough, Nottingham, Kettering, St. Neots, Chacombe (Northants) and London.

There are now only two bell foundries left in the country, that of John Taylor at Loughborough and the Whitechapel foundry in London.

Below: All Saints Oakham bells going for recasting, 1925. Bob Hoy foreground.

Mrs Hoy

HISTORY

Church Bells of Rutland

The founders who cast bells for the churches of Rutland often reproduced their shield or founder's mark on their bells. Examples of which are shown in this article.

A mistake commonly made by founders was to place the letters and dates on the bells either upside down or back to front. A typical one being 'Hew Watts Made Me 1563' at the bottom of the page. This inscription can be found in the treble bell at South Luffenham.

Evidence of 'chip tuning' can be found on many bells in the county. This is the old method by which bells were tuned using a hammer and chisel to remove bell metal in order to change the note of a bell.

The heaviest bell in a peal is called the Tenor and the lightest the Treble. The heaviest bell in Rutland is the Tenor at Oakham. It was originally cast by The Norris Foundry of Stamford in 1677 and inscribed ' God save the King'. In 1875 it was recast by John Taylor of Loughborough. Its diameter is 48.75 inches and it weighs approximately 21cwts.

Several of the Tenor bells have inscriptions relating to death. Because it is the lowest note in a peal the tenor was usually rung at times of mourning or funerals.

Inscriptions

Whissendine Tenor

'My roaring sound doth warning give that men cannot heare always lyve'

Hambleton Tenor

'Non sono Animabus Mortuorum Sed Auribus Viventium'

(I sound not for the souls of the dead but for the ears of the living)

Uppingham Tenor

'Ye ringers all who prize your health and happiness, be sober merry and wise and youll the same possess – Pack and Chapman of London, Walter Robarts Ch. Warden 1772'

Langham Treble

'Grata Sit Arguta Resonans Campanula Voce'

(May the little bell be pleasant sounding with clear tone)

There are only two bells at **Whitwell**, the largest has a rare inscription. The bell is dedicated to **S. Giles** and though there are more than 140 churches dedicated to him in England there are very few bells that bear his name. The inscription reads:

'In: Honore: Sancti: Eiudii'

(In honour of S. Giles)

Bell Stories

● Stories relating to the use and care of bells and towers are many and varied, for example the discovery of the Gunpowder Plot used to be commemorated by a peal of bells at Morcott on November 5th.

● An acre of land at South Luffenham, called Bell Ringing Close, is reputed to have been bought with a legacy left by a lady who used to find her way home by listening for the Curfew bell at eight o'clock. A similar story is connected to Langham.

Old Customs

Many old customs, when the bells used to be rung, have long since ceased to take place. These would have included: Pancake bells, Gleaning bells, Death knells, Curfew bells, Loyalty peals, Meeting bells and a Banns peal.

Bell Ringing Today

Bellringers and friends celebrate New Year's Eve, 1989, in the belfry of All Saints, Oakham.

Brian and Elizabeth Nicholls

● The bells of Rutland can be heard ringing at many churches on Sundays and at other times throughout the year by bands of ringers who in total number around 70, and whose ages can range from 9 to 90.

● The Rutland Branch of Bellringers is affiliated to the Peterborough Diocesan Guild of Church Bellringers. As well as the regular service ringing, the local branch members meet for practices and social activities which take place regularly.

Members also join other ringers from within the Guild, at various times through the year for further ringing and meetings. No previous knowledge or qualifications are required to become a ringer, as free training is given to anyone who is interested.

● For more information read *The Church Bells of Rutland* by Thomas North, 1880 and visit John Taylors Bell Foundry Museum in Loughborough.

Text by Nicholas Meadwell

HISTORY

...the biggest liar in Christendom

That was the unenviable name given to Titus Oates who was born in 1649 in a house – no longer in existence – in Oakham Market Place. Titus was far from being the handsomest of men and it could be that from his earliest years he had determined to take revenge wherever possible for the appearance given him by nature. In his *History of England*, Macaulay describes Titus as having "a short neck, legs uneven like those of a badger, with low forehead as that of a baboon. He had purple cheeks and a monstrous length of chin."

Titus awarded himself a doctorate in Divinity, making up a tale that he had obtained the degree from the University of Salamanca. So he was now a false priest with false qualifications. Back in London he came across the half-crazy Dr Tonge, Rector of St. Michael's. He was busy writing pamphlets designed to "alarm and awaken His Majesty's subjects."

Titus, the born liar, was really at home. He set about inventing a plot comprising a fantastic mixture of facts and lies. He told of underground plans for military action to bring England back to the Catholic Church. The plot has been described as "the most monstrous tissue of grotesque falsehood ever proffered to the credulity of a nation."

Titus claimed the Pope had entrusted the government of England to the Jesuits who had selected Catholic clergy, noblemen and gentlemen for all the highest offices of church and state. The Papists were said to be planning to burn all shipping on the Thames and were to rise up at a given signal to massacre all their Protestant neighbours.

A French army was to land in Ireland and all leading statesmen and clerics in England were to be murdered. The 'Popish Plot' as it became known, included several ways of assassinating the King – by poisoning his medicine, stabbing him and shooting him with silver bullets.

Titus revelled in the alarm he had caused. Almost overnight he had been transformed from a half-starved and despised nobody into a famous citizen hailed as "saviour of the nation". He was provided with palatial lodgings, dressed in silk clothes and followed by admiring crowds.

It was in 1684 that the tide started to turn for this infamous son of Oakham. In 1685 the Duke of York brought a civil action against Titus for defamatory language and the jury awarded massive damages of £100,000. Titus could not pay and was put behind bars.

He was stripped of his canonical habits and was ordered to stand in the pillory on certain days each year for as long as he lived. Worst of all he was ordered to be whipped all the way from Newgate to Tyburn. When he reached the end of his humiliating progress through the streets of London, Titus must have presented a pitiful sight. The whip had six thongs and he received 2,256 lashes. At total of 13,536 stripes.

Nevertheless, Titus survived and continued his villainy in devious ways, finally dying in Axe Yard, Westminster, in 1705.

> 66
> *...a short neck, legs uneven like those of a badger, with low forehead as that of a baboon.*
> 99
> **Macaulay**

If ever a person epitomised Rutland and its unique character it is Jeffrey Hudson. He packed an amazing amount of adventures and achievements into the 63 years which he survived despite being only knee-high to a pony – and a small one at that! Surely Rutland's motto 'Multum in Parvo' applied just as aptly to little Jeffrey.

Born in Oakham in 1619, in the thatched cottage opposite the White Lion Inn, Melton Road, Jeffrey was a disappointment to his normal sized parents who did all they could to keep their young 'freak' out of the public eye.

Jeffrey was born very small and he stayed that way. Forget about people like Tom Thumb! Our Jeffrey was a real record breaker. During his first few years he stretched his way to the height of 18 inches (45 centimetres) and he stayed that way as he reached his teenage years and became a young man.

It was at this height (little more than the seat, of a kitchen chair) that Jeffrey was first taken up to Burley-on-the-Hill where his father worked as a cattle drover for the Duke of Buckingham. It was when Jeffrey was about nine years old that the famous pie incident took place.

King Charles I and Queen Henrietta Maria were visiting the Duke and Duchess of Buckingham and, as a dinner time diversion for the royal couple, it was decided to serve Jeffrey up in a cold pie. Clad in a tiny suit of armour, he climbed into a large pie dish which was then covered with a crust of cold pastry.

Two servants carried the dish to the top table where, much to the amazement and delight of the king and queen and whole assembly, Jeffrey popped up in a shower of crumbs. He pranced along the table top, wielding a tiny sword and with the light from the fire and candles sparkling on his armour.

Queen Henrietta Maria

Text by Eddie Hudson

...the shortest knight in history

Photograph courtesy Richard Clarke

asked that the tiny Oakhamian should accompany the royal cavalcade back to London and so it was that the short man's high life began. In those days dwarfs were much in demand as attractions and entertainers at palaces and big houses.

In fact, the little Oakhamian was still very young when he was made a knight and became Sir Jeffrey, no doubt enjoying the limelight and the necessity for other members of the royal court to address him with his title and respect.

Jeffrey did a lot of courier work for the queen and on his first visit to France he became a great favourite at court, receiving presents to the value of £3,000. The journey home did not go as planned, however. The ship was boarded in the Channel by French pirates who found Jeffrey hiding behind a large candlestick and took him to Dunkirk.

It was while in captivity here that Jeffrey was made to fight a duel with a turkey cock. The fact that Jeffrey eventually got back to England means that he survived the strange fight and the turkey probably ended up as someone's dinner.

The Channel was not a fortunate place for Jeffrey. On another mission to France he was taken prisoner by Turkish pirates and sold as a slave on the Barbary Coast. He was not shown any respect despite his size and he suffered many hardships during a period of hard labour. It took a ransom to regain his freedom and when Jeffrey arrived back in his homeland he found it torn apart by the Civil War.

Amazingly, he was made a captain of the King's Horse and rode into battle, no doubt held steady on a special saddle. He was at the side of Prince Rupert during a charge against Roundheads at Newbury. The skirmish was unsuccessful for the Royalists and Jeffrey was quick to blame a horse whose legs were too long and a sword whose blade was too short. As prince and midget were seen fleeing the battlefield, the cry went up from the Roundheads: 'There goes Prince Rupert and Cock Robin'.

Jeffrey was often at the side of his beloved queen during the troubles and he went with her on a friendly Dutch ship which carried them to France.

They lived in an old palace in the city of Nevers and it was here that Jeffrey was involved in a second, and much more serious, duel. This time his opponent was human!

Jeffrey got back to England and kept his head down untll eventually he returned to Oakham and spent much of his time regaling townsfolk with tales of his adventures. A pension from the Duke of Buckingham helped him to survive.

For some reason when he was 30 Jeffrey doubled in height to three feet (90 centimetres), but that was still no taller than a small child.

Jeffrey survived the great plague which swept the land and, after the Great Fire of London, he was invited to London by Queen Henrietta's son, King Charles ll. It was not a good move.

The capital was in turmoil due to the Popish Plot hatched by Titus Oates. As a Catholic, Jeffrey was a suspect and thrown into prison. He died not long after his release, in 1682.

Text by Eddie Hudson

❝

There goes Prince Rupert and Cock Robin

❞

Left: Portrait of Jeffrey Hudson completed 2 January 1644. Artist unknown. Below: Dwarf's Cottage, Oakham, by Hannah Taylor.

HISTORY

....

Signs of the Past

Top: Stretton by David Millard. Above: Edith Weston by JRH Prophet.

Where do you go when you take a country walk? Over the hills and far away? Down by the riverside? Through ancient tracks and greenways or following the course of an old pilgrim way? Or perhaps you take the lanes and byeways to a typical English village or market town.

The English countryside abounds with such delightful places and they all hold clues to our historic past – sometimes to a very ancient, 'lost-in-the-mists-of-time' kind of history.

The clue to all this is so obvious and such a part of our everyday lives that it may have escaped your notice - for the secret is hidden in the names. Names of rivers, mountains, roads, lanes, villages and towns can tell us a lot about where we live or the places we visit for holidays or outings.

Finding out the meanings of place-names can enhance your enjoyment of the countryside and extend your local knowledge but beware; you may become ensnared in a fascinating study which will lead you into the realms of ancient history, topography and linguistics and before you know it you'll be spending time in libraries and record offices rather than walking in the open air!

However, most keen walkers will know something about local topography and in place-name studies this is very useful information. The oldest place-name elements often relate to topographical features and rivers, hills and valleys hold clues to an ancient British past otherwise lost to view.

Naming rivers

Take some river names for example: Avon is one which recurs; it is the same as the Welsh Afon and the Irish Abhann and means simply 'river'. Thames is another fascinating name, recorded as Tamesis by Julius Caesar in 51BC, it means 'dark water' and corresponds to the Sanskrit word Tamasa – the

name of a tributary of the river Ganges.

Names such as these were established in ancient British times for which we have no records other than a few references in later annals and histories and the knowledge gained from modern scholarship.

Other place-names developed in a slightly less remote though still far distant past and contain the elements of Roman, Anglo-Saxon, Danish and Norman settlement.

Settlement by invaders was a gradual process of expansion over hundreds of years. Early Anglo-Saxon settlements were often near the coast or in river valleys close to the waterways which enabled these explorers to reach inland Britain. But as time went on further waves of invaders arrived and the original settlers were pushed further inland or absorbed by the newcomers. All this had an effect on place-names as new elements were added to existing ones.

Rutland's place-names reveal strong Anglo-Saxon elements whereas across the county boundaries you can find Roman, Danish and Norman elements which are few and far between in Rutland.

The Roman road – Ermine Street built to connect London and Lincoln – now the A1, cuts through the north eastern corner of Rutland.

Stamford, the beautiful market town on the eastern border of Rutland, despite its position on Ermine Street, was never a Roman town. It grew up as the stane (stone) ford an important crossing of the river Welland - and its origins are Saxon and Danish.

However Casterton a few miles over the Rutland border was a Roman site where a village grew up beside the fort which offered it protection. The name derives from the OE Ceaster – a loan word from the Latin Castra – a city or walled town that had been a Roman Station- this is the same element found in

Ancient spring at Ashwell

Melton and Rutland Journal

Place-name Elements

OE – Old English
ON – Old Norse
OD – Old Danish
L – Latin

broc (OE) – brook/stream
burgh (OE) – a fortified place
burna (OE) – a stream/spring
by (ON) – a farmstead/village
dael (OE) – a valley
dun (OE) – a hill
ham (OE) – settlement/village
holt (OE) – wood/thicket
hyl (OE) – hill
hyrst (OE) – hillock/copse
leah (OE) – clearing in a wood
Magna (L) – great
Parva (L) – small
stede (OE) – a place
straet (OE) – a Roman road
thorpe (OD) – a secondary settlement
toft (OD) – enclosure
tun (OE) – farmstead/village
wald (OE) – woodland/wold
wic (OE) – dairy farm
worth (OE) – enclosure

Chester, the famous Roman city in north west England.

Saxon settlement followed the withdrawal of the Roman legions in the late 5th century and Rutland place-names attest considerable Saxon influence within the bounds of the old county.

Close to the A1 is the village of Stretton – the tun or settlement on the straet Old English (OE) for street or road. This a common village name found all over the country and always associated with Roman roads.

Domesday Book

This information could be described as topographical and other examples can be found. Market Overton was recorded in Domesday book (DB) as Overtune the settlement on the slope or ridge. The Market is a later addition but was known to exist in the 12th century.

Nearby Thistleton was once a very important Romano-British site on the border of tribal territories. The name means the village where the thistles grow. This may not sound very exciting but thistles and nettles are an indication of habitation and this name may signify that the Saxon settlers who named the village, knew that other people had been there before them.

The elements ham and ton refer to settlement in the early Anglo-Saxon period, probably by the 7th century in Rutland. Both translate roughly as village, settlement, or homestead, with the names in ham probably the earlier.

These endings are sometimes joined to a personal name – that of the tribal leader who brought his people to found the village. So we have Clipsham (Clyp's ham), a Roman villa site close to the A1. Oakham (Occa's ham) now the county town.

Because of its small size Rutland can easily be explored and the area around Rutland Water is excellent for walking. Hambleton (DB Hameldun) translates as village near a hill – dun being OE for hill and hamol OE for maimed which may mean treeless or bare.

Hambleton was a royal manor belonging to Queen Edith, wife of Edward the Confessor. She is commemorated in the nearby village of Edith Weston (the west tun) and is known to have held possessions in Rutland at the time of the Norman Conquest.

Morcott another village near Rutland Water means the cot (cottage or hut) on the moor or wasteland, Cottesmore, in the north of the county is similar but includes the personal name of Cott.

Wardley, on a hill overlooking the Eyebrook which forms the south western boundary of Rutland, combines the OE weard (watch) and leah (open place in woodland) and is believed to have been a lookout or watch point

Whitwell (DB Witewell) translates as Hwit (white) Wella (spring or stream). There is a small stream here and the place was once considered sacred. The church now stands on this site – a not uncommon event since, in the early days of Christianity, churches often grew up on previously pagan sites. The holy pagan place then became absorbed into the new Christian religion.

Understanding place-names may not be easy but it is always fascinating. With a little time and trouble a pattern may emerge which will reflect the ways of the ancient inhabitants of your area.

This world may have gone for ever but the villages and towns remain – changed beyond recognition but still containing within their names and landscapes a link to the past waiting for those who have the patience to discover it.

Text by Carol Debney, Country Walking Magazine

Mr A. P. F. Chapman who represented Oakham School and Uppingham School at cricket and went on to captain England at the age of 25.

1967, the first official Rutland County Cricket Club team to take to the field since 1886. Back row left to right: M. Catchpole, R. Kelsey, G. Nickerson, A. Earl, D. Martin; front row left to right: L. Ellis, D. Meadows, G. Cooper, I. Balfour (Captain), P. Bagshaw and P. White.

HISTORY

From Village

The County of Rutland has a remarkable cricketing history. The first mention of cricket, which connected Rutland to the game was in 1786. But it was in 1790, when the population of England and Wales was, approximately only 8,675,000, and that of Rutland 15,000, when the first recorded match took place in the County.

It was on the 19th, 20th, and 21st of July, at Burley-on-the-Hill, which was the seat of George Finch, the 9th Earl of Winchilsea, who had been the founder of MCC in 1787, and who, in that first game, captained All England versus Hampshire for 1,000 guineas. All England, 92 and 103, losing to Hampshire, 135 and 61 for the loss of 3 wickets, by 7 wickets.

The Napoleonic Wars took their toll of the game, but in 1808 the first match under the name of Rutland was played, again at Burley-on-the-Hill, and headed by the Earl of Winchilsea, against 11 of the Military from Norman Cross, which "was decided in favor of the former, they having one innings and 23 notches to spare".

In the years that followed the game spread round the County and in 1815

Uppingham School played Oakham School for the first time, but in 1826 George Finch, the father of Rutland cricket, died, and the interest which he had created in the game tended to lull.

In 1854, however, 22 of Uppingham and District played 11 of All England at Uppingham. A similar match followed in 1857, and in 1859 22 of Oakham and District played 11 of All England at Oakham.

Interest in the game continued to increase through the 1870s, H. H. Stephenson, who captained England to Australia on the first tour of that country in 1861–1862, was appointed as the Professional at Uppingham School in 1872.

Though there was no official Rutland County Cricket Club, County matches were played more and more frequently through that decade until, in 1881, the first Rutland County Cricket Club was formed, in which year Rutland played MCC at Lord's for the first time.

The match between MCC and Ground versus Rutland at Lord's in 1885 created a record at the time. MCC and Ground batted first and at luncheon they had

scored 226 for 5 wickets. Their innings finished at 3.30 pm with their total score at 278, J. Furley taking 4 wickets for 73 runs and H. Drake 3 wickets for 56 runs. At the close of play on the first day Rutland had scored 207 for the loss of 6 wickets, with H. Drake having scored 67 and J. Furley 56.

On the second day Rutland were all out for 209, which was followed by M.C.C. and Ground scoring 643 for 8 wickets, in 5 hours and 35 minutes, there being no declarations in those days, they batted to the close of play. So on that second day, 645 runs were scored for the loss of 12 wickets, surpassing by exactly 100 runs the previous record for one day's batting at Lord's.

The Rutland County Cricket Club was dissolved in 1887, but the feats of two of the outstanding players of the time, J. Furley, who played for England, and H. Drake, continued as before, and they were later joined by R. N. Douglas, who played for the Gentlemen of England and, for a short time, A. O. Jones, who later captained England.

In 1896 these four combined together in a remarkable match when Rutland

The LAWS of CRICKET,

Revised at the STAR and GARTER, PALL-MALL, *Feb.* 25th, 1784,

By a Committee of NOBLEMEN and GENTLEMEN

Of *Kent, Hampshire, Surrey, Suffex, Middlesex,* and *London.*

The BALL
MUST weigh no less than five ounces and a half, nor more than five ounces and three quarters.
It cannot be changed during the game, but with consent of both parties.

The BAT
Must not exceed four inches an l one quarter in the widest part.

The STUMPS
Must be twenty-two inches, the ball six inches long.

The BOWLING-CREASE
parallel with the stumps, three feet in length, with
CREASE

The STRIKER
Is out, If the ball is bowled off, or the stump bowled out of the ground.
Or if the ball, from a stroke over or under his bat, or upon his hands (but not wrists) is held before it touches the ground, though it be hugged to the body of the catcher.
Or if, in striking, both his feet are over the popping crease, and his wicket is put down, except his bat is grounded within it:
Or if he runs out of his ground to hinder a catch :
Or if a ball is struck up, and he wilfully strikes it
Or if, in running a notch, the wicket
t row, or with the ball in hand
is grounded over the
stump must be

6. If the ball is struck up, the striker may guard his wicket, either with his bat or with his body.
In single wicket matches, if the striker moves out of his ground to strike at the ball, he shall be allowed no notch for such stroke.

The WICKET-KEEPER
Shall stand at a reasonable distance behind the wicket, and shall not move till the ball is out of the bowler's hand, and shall not, by any noise incommode the striker; and if his hands, knees, foot, or head, be over or before the wicket, though the ball hit it, it shall not be out.

Above: An extract from the 1784 Laws of Cricket found in the Finch Manuscripts at Burley.

Left: 1967, the second official Rutland County Cricket Club team to take to the field since 1886. Back row left to right: I. Balfour (Captain), D. Wright, G. Nickerson, A. Earl, R. Smith, R. Partridge, B. Nickerson; Front row left to right: J. Smith, P. Shakeshaft, B. Earl and F. Hinch.

to County

played Four Counties at Uppingham. Four Counties, in their first innings, were dismissed for 128, W F. Neilson opening the batting and carrying his bat for 47 not out, J. Furley taking 3 wickets for 34 runs, H. Drake 4 wickets for 37 runs, A. O. Jones 3 wickets for 39 runs.

In reply, at the end of the first day, Rutland had scored 331 for 2 wickets, J. Furley 129, and A. O. Jones, 113, putting on 212 for the first wicket partnership.

On the second day Rutland took their score to 603 for 2 wickets before declaring, H. Drake, 189 not out, and R. N. Douglas, 148 not out, putting on 315 in an unbroken third wicket partnership, 272 of those runs being scored in only two hours on the second morning.

Four Counties, in their second innings, scored 167, W. F. Neilson again carrying his bat and scoring 100 not out, J. Furley taking 3 wickets for 47 runs, H. Drake 3 wickets for 49 runs, and A. O. Jones 4 wickets for 45 runs. The wicket-keeper, R. N. Douglas, helped to dismiss 9 of the opposition in the match, and Rutland won by an innings and 308 runs.

The first Rutland Cricket League was formed in 1897, and interest in the game

continued to increase until the First World War after which, until the Second World War, cricket thrived with even the smallest hamlets having teams. Quite a few Rutland cricketers were to make their name in the game, and R. Tyler, the professional at Oakham School who played in League Cricket, H. C. Snary, A. P. F. Chapman, who captained England, J. C. Bradshaw, W. H. Bradshaw and C. L. Edgson, were outstanding, the last five named all playing First Class cricket.

Occasional Rutland matches were played, though there was still no official County Club, and in 1935 the first First Class County match in Rutland was played on Oakham School's ground, Leicestershire playing Kent.

After the Second World War, the first Rutland County Youth XI played representative matches in 1950, and in 1951 the Rutland Boys' Cricket Association was formed. Once more Rutland was to see a number of notable cricketers, with R. C. Smith playing in the First Class game, and again a few unofficial Rutland matches were played.

In 1960, I founded the Rutland County Youth Cricket Association. In 1964, I re-

formed the Rutland County Cricket Club. In 1967, I founded the Rutland County Cricket Association, which became the first Constituent Member of the National Cricket Association, with Mr. D. C. S. Compton, CBE, becoming the Patron, and in 1986, I founded the Rutland County Schools' Cricket Association. In 1974, at the time of Local Government Reorganisation, I successfully argued that Rutland should stay a separate County, cricketwise, and may that status permanently remain.

© Extracts from a book, *The History of Rutland Cricket*, to be published by Ian Balfour

View through the North Gates towards the site of the original Burley-on-the-Hill cricket ground (1790).

HISTORY

Lord Lonsdale & the Belt

Leicester Mercury

Lord Lonsdale. His fresh daily gardenia and six inch long cigar were characteristic of this extravagant personality who was once described as 'almost an Emperor and not quite a gentleman'.

Fact File

● The 5th Earl of Lonsdale was born in London in 1857 but lived much of his life at Barleythorpe Hall, Rutland.

● He was the so-called Yellow Earl because of the yellow livery he gave to his carriages and servants.

● He was the man behind the world-famous boxing trophy the Lonsdale Belt and a founding father of the Automobile Association, hence the yellow livery of its cars and vans.

● A prominent figure in hunting and horse racing, he was master of the hunts at Quorn, Cottesmore and Pytchley and also chief steward with the Jockey Club.

● He travelled extensively in the US and Canada collecting specimens in Alaska for the Scottish Naturalist Society.

● He died at the Stud House at Barleythorpe – now Lonsdale House part of Rutland Sixth Form College – in 1944.

The Lonsdale Belt

British Boxing Board of Control

Below: Catmose Cottage, Oakham, once the home of Lord and Lady Lonsdale.

Instituted by the National Sporting Club in 1909 and paid for by Lord Lonsdale. A boxer who wins the Belt three times at the same weight keeps it and is entitled to a pension. The first outright winner was Jim Driscoll in 1911. In 1976 the pension was discontinued. Originally the Belts were made in 9 carat gold.

Susanna Lawson

COMMUNITY

The Hunt

The Hunt

Tally-Ho, Tally-Ho
Scarlet jackets come and go
Over the ancient dry stone wall
Horses gallop, sweat, some fall,
And some don't try to jump at all.

Across the fields they race and run,
Cares forgotten in the fun.
I hear the hounds, they bark and bay,
As ever nearer to their prey
They close,in frantic, all-out chase.

In vain the fox tries to outpace
The pitiless hoard, till at the kill
These country 'sportsmen' watch their fill
To see its body torn apart
The culmination of their 'Art'.

I wonder, as their horse they box,
If they are glad they're not the fox.

Gerald Botteley

Leicester Mercury

Above: View of Cottesmore Hunt in Uppingham Market Place from the Falcon Inn. More than 300 people watch the Christmas Meet set off.

Andrew Jenkins

Left: 1910. A large crowd has gathered to watch the Meet of the Cottesmore Hunt, probably at Burley-on-the-Hill. The Cottesmore can trace its history back to 1728. Lord Lonsdale on the horse at centre.

73

Oakham School

Left: Oakham
School Crest

Right: Entrance
to the School from
Market Place

The 16th century priest was often a man of position, wealth and influence. He was probably not without charity, an interest in education and a certain sense of self-interest.

Archdeacon Robert Johnson (1541-1625) was no exception and he established in Rutland a number of charitable institutions which would preserve his name and ensure countless acts of thanksgiving throughout eternity.

Five of these charities survive today and include two major independent schools; in Uppingham a school and an almshouse (Hospital of Christ) and in Oakham an almshouse, a Hospital of St. John and St. Anne, and Oakham School.

The official date for the founding of Oakham School is 1584, the original building surviving today to the north of the parish church. There was, presumably, a school in Oakham before this but Robert Johnson's foundation is fairly described as the first free school in the county town.

The Old School

The earliest pupils would, of course, have been male and residents of Oakham and its immediate environs. There would, however, have been opportunities and, considering the small size of the local population, a need for boarding pupils who would have lodged in the town.

It is unlikely that there was any building designed specifically for boarders before the mid-18th century. The syllabus of the 16th century would have consisted entirely of Latin, Greek and Hebrew.

For nearly 200 years there must have been little outward or internal change, though the School prospered financially.

Visitor Reception and Bursar's Office

Present Day

It was announced in March 1970 that the School would cease to accept the Direct Grant on September 1, 1970. There followed the first Appeal to Old Oakhamians and parents, increased emphasis on boarding to replace the diminishing 11 plus pupils and in 1971.........girls.

Seventeen boarders and 10 day-girls aged between 13 and 16 arrived in September 1971 and spent their first year based in College House.

Within 12 months the Round House had been completed to provide accommodation for 60 girl boarders. By 1989 the number of girls in the School had reached 50 per cent in nearly all age groups. Oakham had become one of the few truly co-educational schools in the independent sector.

Such an increase in numbers demanded an increase in facilities to accommodate the pupils, but mere increase was not seen to be sufficient. The Headmaster and Trustees were determined to build to high standards structurally and aesthetically and to provide pupils with a wide range of opportunities in all aspects of non-academic life.

In its emphasis on co-education, the Arts, especially music, whole-hearted adoption of computer technology and an innovative academic syllabus, Oakham stresses the advantages of current educational thinking.

Through its seven-day working week, retention of pupils' uniforms, competitive games, and its succession of architectural styles, Oakham retains much of what is best from the past.

Round House, Oakham School

Text and photographs by Roger Blackmore

Uppingham School

The historic buildings of Uppingham School should not lead the observer who admires their antiquity to imagine that today's Uppingham sleeps in some cosy time-warp.

The great Victorian Headmaster, Edward Thring, was also a great pioneer. Under his guidance, Uppingham became the first School in Britain to have a gymnasium, to have modern languages taught as a compulsory part of the curriculum,

and by native speakers.

The School had the first Director of Music, Paul David, a family friend of Mendelssohn, and the musical tradition he established continues and flourishes to this day.

Uppingham was described by *The Independent* newspaper recently as a school that has 'never been afraid to challenge orthodoxy'. In recent times the challenge of information technology has led the school to establish facilities that would be the

envy of many a university: 'A' level design was pioneered here, and the school is about to build a fine new multi-media centre for the teaching of art, design and technology to replace the Thring Centre, which was one of the earliest in this field nearly thirty years ago. A fine new maths block was opened recently by Professor Stephen Hawking.

Among other developments taking the school into the twenty-first century is the opening of a third girls'

The School Room and Chapel at Uppingham.

today

sixth-form house in September 1994, a new sixth-form centre, and the opening of a new facility for day-pupils from the age of 11.

Members of the school and of the local community enjoy the use of the school's splendid theatre, and the sports centre, opened as long ago as 1972.

Uppingham remains a warm and friendly school: it retains the values of its past, while preparing its pupils for the world of the future. It is still, in Thring's words, 'A blessed place to grow up in.'

Text by David Gaine

77

HISTORIC BUILDINGS OF UPPINGHAM SCHOOL

Drawings & Text by Warwick Metcalfe

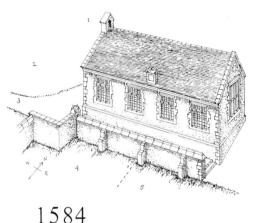

1. Original Schoolroom
2. Churchyard
3. Footpath to Hospital
4. Town pound for stray livestock
5. Beast Hill
6. Usher's room, or little grammar school c.1836
7. East window replaced by fireplace C17
8. Cottage built against E wall-C18 or early C19
9. Cottage and fireplace removed & E window restored 1956.
10. Upper storey added to Usher's room 1964.

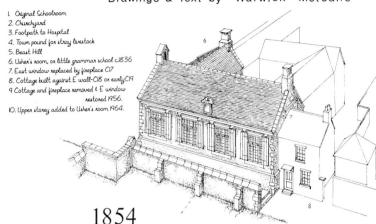

1584

1854

THE ELIZABETHAN SCHOOL

The reign of Elizabeth I, was the first great age of school building. Henry VIII's dissolution of the monasteries put an end to the rare opportunities for learning open to laymen, and left nothing in their place. But his daughter's accession introduced a period of stability and prosperity, and the rise of a wealthy new class of traders and merchants, amongst who, were certain public spirited citizens, far sighted enough to found schools and hospitals. The former, so called with the object of schooling boys in the rudiments of writing and grammar in their mother tongue, together with Latin and Greek - a passport to Oxford on Cambridge.

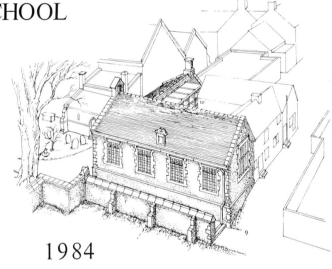

1984

1592

Whilst the Grammar schools provided for the young, the Hospitals attended to the needs of the old, supplying shelter and security for the aged who might otherwise be destitute. Many well known schools owe their origin to the enlightened patrons of this period, but few are fortunate enough to have any, let alone all the original buildings erected by their founder, intact and still in use, four centuries later.. Yet in the words of its founder Archdeacon Johnson, 'by God's Grace' this is what has happened at Uppingham. Here, within the complex of many different buildings in different styles which have accompanied Uppingham's expansion to meet the demands of developments in education over 400 years, the venerable heritage from which it grew may be observed, still in daily use.

1. Main Hospital with dormitories over.
2. Warden's House.
3. Kitchen and outbuildings.
4. Chapel
5. Hospital Yard, formerly a pasture.
6. Hospital, later School Lane.
7. Old 'Jitty' (passageway)
8. Sloping site on South side, formerly a 'Conygree' or rabbit warren.
9. Path, later cobbled, became cause of dispute between school and town.

THE ELIZABETHAN HOSPITAL

1825

1. Drawing room 1796

2. Stoops at end of School Lane.

3. Original Chapel, was also School House dining hall, raised with 2 dormitories over and cupola 1825.

4. Twenty one studies built between 1783 and 1811.

5. Garden layout according to 1839 town map.

The Schoolmaster was also the Warden of the Hospital. The Scholarships the Founder had established for Oxford and Cambridge, attracted pupils from further than Uppingham, and it soon became evident the Schoolmaster could supplement his salary by boarding pupils in the Hospital, and charging for their keep. By about 1620 the old men for whom it was intended, had agreed instead to live with relatives, but continue to receive their stipends from Johnson's charity. The arrangement suited all parties involved and the hospital became the School House, in which the boarders were accommodated, the Chapel serving as the Hall. By 1825, dormitories had been built over the Hall, studies built along the east and north boundaries of the yard, and a new drawing room added to the West end of the Master's house.

1854

2. Triple-arched School Gate with wooden doors 1829.

3. Three extra studies added 1846.

1. Bedroom over drawing room 1832.

4. Chapel/Hall extended eastward with third dormitory over.

5. Original Hospital/School House extended by extra bay and dormer 1840.

Thring arrived to begin his transformation in 1853, by which time further changes had taken place and the site developed to its maximum extent. In future any further expansion would need to take place elsewhere. By now an extra bedroom had been added over the Headmaster's sitting room at the west end, and an additional bay accommodating a sixth form room had been added to the east end of the former hospital. The hall and dormitories had also been extended eastwards, the studies now covered the entire extent of the northern boundary and an arched entrance with wooden doors replaced the 'stoops' leading into school lane.

1992

10. New Buttery and Music School extension 1980.

By the time Thring died, numbers in the school had risen to well over 300. A new school Hall and Chapel had been built and there were 10 boarding houses. The tercentenary of original Hospital building was therefore taken as an opportunity to end its role as the boarding house, by moving its pupils to a new school house on a site further west. The former Master's House then became the Master's Common Room, the Hall which had meanwhile been further extended became extra classrooms, whilst the Hospital was gutted and transformed into the school library. In 1949 the Hall was gutted to form the 1939-45 war memorial and extension to the library.

Illustrations by J.P.W. Metcalfe

oyal Air Force Cottesmore has a long and varied history dating back to pre-World War II. It has generally been host to bomber or training units apart from a period between 1943 and 1945 when it was under the control of the United States Army Air Force operating in a troop carrying role. The version of Tornado now based at Cottesmore is a strike/attack aircraft and so the the unit is continuing in its tradition of training bomber aircrews.

Types of aircraft which have operated from Cottesmore include the Fairey Battle, Vickers Wellesley, Handley Page Hampden and Hereford, Bristol Beaufighter, de Havilland Mosquito and Avro Lancaster, all piston engined bombers.

The United States Army Air Force flew Dakotas, sometimes towing gliders on their operations. To train student pilots during the six years between 1948 and 1954 de Havilland Tiger Moth, Percival Prentice, North American Harvard and Boulton Paul Balliol aircraft were flown from Cottesmore.

Cottesmore's entry into the jet age was via the English Electric Canberra followed by Handley Page Victors and Avro Vulcans. Armstrong Whitworth Argosies also operated from the unit between 1969 and 1976 in the radar calibration role.

Tornado arrived in 1980 and the Tri-National Tornado Training Establishment was formally opened in early 1981. The first crews from the three participating nations, when converted to the aircraft, were employed as instructors. More than 2,200 aircrew have been trained and many, after a tour of duty with their national squadrons, have returned to Cottesmore as instructors.

COMMUNITY

The RAF in

Open Day at Cottesmore

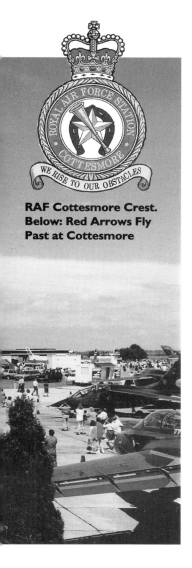

**RAF Cottesmore Crest.
Below: Red Arrows Fly
Past at Cottesmore**

TTTE Crest

**Right: A Vulcan
B2 Cottesmore
Wing dropping
21,000lb bombs
in 1965.**

**Below: Paratroops of the
82nd Airborne Division
board aircraft of the
316th Troop Carrier
Group on 17th
September 1944.**

Rutland

Planes of To-day...

> **❝
> On 17th
> September 1944
> Sunday morning
> worshippers on
> their way to
> church could
> hear the distant
> rumble of aero
> engines. On the
> airfield the
> biggest armada
> of aircraft yet
> seen in Rutland
> moved out of
> their dispersals
> and rolled
> towards the take
> off point like so
> many
> disciplined bees.
> ❞**

From the *Green Fields and
the Sky, The History of RAF
Cottesmore* by N.J.
Roberson and J.G. Tallis.

**Left: Italian,
German and
British Tornadoes
in flight.**

The Evolution of an Airfield

1938

In the early days the airfield had few buildings and a rolled, grassed area (left). By 1953 there were three concrete runways including the extended main runway for jets. In the 1980s the Station had become highly complex with a huge servicing area, hangers and a small township.

1953

Above: American Memorial Stone at RAF Cottesmore

**RAF North
Luffenham
Crest**

**One of the famous planes which flew from
North Luffenham before flying ceased in 1963.**

The Ground Radio Servicing Centre is the Station's main role to-day,
responsible for servicing many different radars all over the world. RAF
North Luffenham also has the Radio Technical Publications Squadron which
produces many technical manuals associated with radar. Also, the Ground
Radio Engineering Development Investigation Team solve complex technical
problems which arise in ground radio equipment. RAF North Luffenham is
threatened with closure at present.

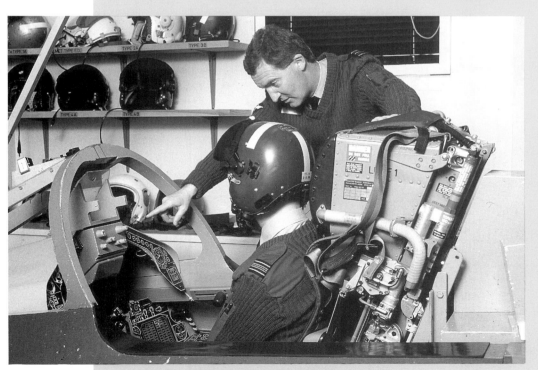

**The Aviation Medicine Training Centre prepares
aircrew for situations which may be a little unusual.**

Text and photographs RAF Cottesmore and North Luffenham, N.J. Roberson and J.G. Tallis

Railway Mania!

For almost 100 years the mining of iron ore by opencast methods was an important industry in Rutland. Rutland Railway Museum began in 1979 at Cottesmore with the aim of preserving various aspects of railways in industry and ironstone railways in particular.

The Museum is home to an extensive collection of industrial steam and diesel locomotives together with a large assortment of other rolling stock.

The Museum is normally open at weekends for static viewing with a number of operating days throughout the summer when rides are available together with refreshment and gift shop facilities. Demonstration freight trains and shunting operations may also take place on these days.

Rutland Railway Museum is run by a small band of enthusiasts who are all volunteers giving up what spare time they can to help preserve a part of the country's heritage. New members are welcome.

Below: Former Colsterworth Quarries Loco 1382 with Museum chairman David Atkinson and well known historian Eric Tonks.

Above: Singapore. The Museum's ex Royal Navy Singapore Dockyard Loco. A member of the Far Eastern Prisoner of War Association (FEPOW) whose crests are carried on the cab side. Seen here on a busy open day during 1988.

Tank engine 'Salmon', built by Andrew Barclay in 1942, giving rides.

NO ENGINE TO PASS THIS BOARD WITHOUT PERMISSION FROM THE SHUNTER

Photographs and text compiled by Richard Knight

A traction engine and a steam roller visiting the Museum during one of the early steam open days.

COMMUNITY
Railway Models

The worlds of engineering and art meet in the skills of Whissendine teacher Peter Smith who recreates the golden age of steam in miniature. He makes models, not of locomotives but railway buildings such as signal boxes, trackside goods sheds, booking halls and complete stations for enthusiasts who install them on their own layouts.

Almost all the models are based on actual buildings. They are feather board shell, finished in intricate detail internally and externally, with fixtures such as tiny gas lamps and trailing ivy.Peter also constructs items ranging from a level-crossing keeper's cottage to a shop, pub or chapel.

One of his largest constructions was a model of the station at Wells-next-the-Sea, Norfolk, six feet long by two-and-a-half feet. Another is based on the style of the Severn-Wye Railway in the 1890s with several sidings.

Kirtley Models, the name of his business, was taken from Matthew Kirtley, 19th century railway engineer, much admired by Peter.

There is no doubt that Peter's work involves skills as varied as woodworking, electronics, metalwork and technical drawing as well as unlimited enthusiasm. And all this is quietly going on in a small Rutland village!

The illustrations show examples of Peter Smith's work.

Photographs by Peter Smith

HISTORY

....

Old Picture Postcards

Barrowden in the 1870s

1905 Published by Dolby Bros., Stamford.

An interesting postcard of Barrowden made from an old photograph taken during the construction of the Peterborough to Rugby railway line in the 1870s. A contractor's locomotive is shown crossing the newly built viaduct over the River Welland, and Barrowden Church can be seen in the background.

Andrew Jenkins

Andrew Jenkins

Manton Station

1923
Published by Stocks, Uppingham.

This busy junction station was sited away from the village, at the southern end on Manton tunnel. It was mainly used for transferring passengers between the Oakham – Kettering and Oakham – Peterborough lines. Although the station was closed in the 1960s the lines are still used and the buildings, now part of an industrial estate, are still largely intact.

Seaton Viaduct

Circa 1925
Unknown publisher.

The impressive Seaton Viaduct crossing the Welland Valley with Harringworth in the distance. It is nearly three quarters of a mile long and made up of 82 arches up to 70 feet high. Two thousand navvies were employed on its construction from 1878 to 1882. The workers' camp, known as 'Cyprus' was built on the fields in the foreground of this picture.

David Griffiths

HISTORY

Old Picture Postcards

Andrew Jenkins

Electioneering

January 1906
Unknown publisher.

The Liberal candidate, Harold Pearson, about to set out on an electioneering trip in the 1906 General Election. This photograph was taken in London Road, outside the Uppingham National School which has now been demolished.

Andrew Jenkins

Preston Windmill

1904
Unknown publisher.

This is the old post mill which stood near the Ridlington Road. It was used until 1925 and partly demolished the following year. Although there is no trace of it now, it was not until about 1950 that the round house, on which the mill stood, was finally demolished.

Andrew Jenkins

'I am enjoying myself at Oakham'

1910
Published by Birn Bros., London.

A typical Edwardian comic postcard which was overprinted for use in various towns around the country.

Reaping

Circa 1905
Published by S Cooke, Hambleton

This and the following two postcards are from a series published by the Hambleton schoolmaster and photographer Mr S Cooke. They record in marvellous detail, turn of the century farming scenes in the area around the village.

Andrew Jenkins

Andrew Jenkins

Evening

Circa 1905
Published by S Cooke, Hambleton

Waiting for Milk

Circa 1905
Published by S Cooke, Hambleton

Andrew Jenkins

COMMUNITY

Rutland at War

1914-18

Because Rutland was such a small county it was possible, in 1920, to compile a record of all those who took part in the Great War, parish by parish. There was a review of Rutland's involvement, biographies of the fallen, rolls of honour village by village, civilian and school contributions were noted as well as many more aspects. This book, *Rutland and the Great War*, must have been the finest record assembled in England, illustrated as it was by photographs of almost all the combatants.

Presentation copies were given to many families. The book became a treasured possession.

'One thing this record proves. Rutland did her duty. In comparison with the rest of the country she sent 35 per cent of her male population to the war, against 25 per cent for the whole country. Of the men of Rutland who went to war, 14 per cent were killed or died from wounds, against 12 per cent for the United Kingdom.'

Buckingham Palace
29th November, 1915

Sir,

I have the honour to inform you that the King has heard with much interest that you have at the present moment seven sons serving in His Majesty's Forces.

I am commanded to express to you The King's congratulations and to assure you that His Majesty much appreciates the spirit of patriotism which prompted this example, in one family, of loyalty and devotion to their Sovereign and Empire.

I have the honour to be,
Sir,
Your obedient Servant,
F M Ponsonby
Keeper of the Privy Purse

Top: The Scott Family of Soldier Sons. Above: George V sent his congratulations early in the war to Mr Scott. Below: Each book had a Presentation Book Plate

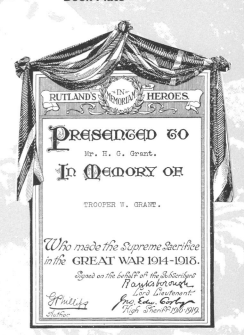

School War Records

Uppingham

Old Boys who served in H M Forces	2500
Killed in action or died of wounds	451
Victoria Crosses	4
Military Crosses	267
Distinguished Service Orders	88
Foreign Orders	59
Mentioned in Dispatches	574
Other honours	82

Oakham

then a smaller establishment
had the following record:

Old Boys who served in H M Forces	390
Killed in action or died of wounds	62
Military Crosses	35
Distinguished Service Orders	10
Foreign Orders	11
Mentioned in Dispatches	60
Other honours	70

Evacuees 1939

Wartime evacuees from Maynard Road School, Walthamstow, at Langham

E R

I WISH TO MARK, BY THIS PERSONAL MESSAGE, my appreciation of the service you have rendered to your Country in 1939.

In the early days of the War you opened your door to strangers who were in need of shelter, & offered to share your home with them.

I know that to this unselfish task you have sacrificed much of your own comfort, & that it could not have been achieved without the loyal co-operation of all in your household.

By your sympathy you have earned the gratitude of those to whom you have shown hospitality, & by your readiness to serve you have helped the State in a work of great value.

Elizabeth R

Mrs. Stafford Smith.

Wartime Langham – An Evacuee Remembers

I arrived as an eight-year-old from Walthamstow in September 1939 and stayed four years in the village. I can't recall the journey but remember waiting in the Village Institute to be selected by a potential foster parent, and the excitement on waking next morning and looking from my bedroom window to see Staff Smith's farmyard spread out below me.

I remember the near certainty of at least two feet of persistent snow every winter (22° of frost on 19th January, 1940) and the total freezing of our 'unspillable' inkwells at the Scout Hut, our first temporary school. Later we graduated to the Village Institute and finally Oakham Central School where I was terrified by the headmaster, Mr Cartwright.

For the first time I saw hams curing on the kitchen walls, new born lambs and the embarrassed Local Defence Volunteers being put through their rigorous drill routines. I remember vividly tree-climbing, bird nesting, fishing for newts in the 'pit', netting sticklebacks in the brook, sledging in the rifle range, jumping contests over the brook at Cold Overton road and scrambling over 'The Gun' in Well Street (before it was removed to be melted down for the war effort).

I was allowed into the Oakham signal box and I sang in the church choir where Dulcie Ellingworth was choirmistress. I recall Mr Tidd's village shop and his competitor, Mr Stacey's emporium; listening to pearls of wisdom from the old hump-backed roadsweeper Sonny Edwards; the long summers, teas in the hayfield; ratcatching at threshing time; Barton's bus trips to Oakham and Melton markets, and a host of other events.

Adolf Hitler spread very little goodwill intentionally but he accidentally gave me a million happy memories!

Terry Weeden

COMMUNITY

A Country Newspaper

Providing information, entertainment and, above all, a service to the community. These should be the functions of a local newspaper, and that's the constant aim of the *Rutland Times* which, in less than two decades, has become very much a part of the Rutland scene.

It is sometimes suggested that a relatively small, local publication is simply an organ for parish pump news. Of course, it does provide a look at the everyday life that goes on in local towns and villages.

Rutland has often been praised, and envied, for its community spirit. That spirit is reflected in the interest in and concern for their fellow citizens by the people of Rutland. And that is why these people are always eager to greet their 'friend' bringing the news each week – the *Rutland Times*.

But the newspaper, which is read by so many Rutland residents and is also sent regularly to numerous places throughout Britain and the rest of the world, contains much more than local gossip. Reports from the courts and councils are always read with interest as are weddings, obituaries, anniversaries, dramatic reviews, criminal activities. In fact, the whole spectrum of local life is in its pages.

And, of course, the *Times* covers all special events on the Rutland calendar, like the Rutland Agricultural Society Show, the mini-marathon, Oakham Festival and countless items dealing with village fetes, school sports days, sports of all kinds, sponsored events, etc. If it happens in and around Rutland the *Rutland Times* likes to think it covers it. It also examines controversial topics and provides a voice for the public as can be seen by the number of readers' letters.

It's all a long way (though not in time) since the *Rutland Times* first hit the streets. It was early in 1977 that two teachers at the Vale of Catmose College (Chris Cooter and Chris Olney) and an employee of the *Leicester Mercury* (David Kleinman) decided over a pint in The Wheatsheaf,

Oakham, that Rutland needed its own 'independent community newspaper'.

A few weeks later, in April of that year, Issue Number One of the *Rutland Times* appeared. The main story and picture on the front page was the one hundredth birthday of a marvellous old local lady, Annie Withers.

Headlines in the May edition of the then monthly newspaper was the resignation of the Uppingham Parish Council chairman, Tom Dorman, over the 'yellow lines controversy'.

In the next edition the little production team really had something into which to get its teeth - the Silver Jubilee of Queen Elizabeth ll. They marked the occasion with a page of pictures of Her Majesty's previous visit to the county.

Since those early days a lot has happened to the *Rutland Times*. First it went fortnightly and then weekly. Then, from being a free newspaper pushed through doors, it went paid-for. Rutlanders showed their desire for their own newspaper by becoming regular subscribers and the *Rutland Times* has continued to grow in size, circulation and stature.

Yet, still the people of Rutland regard it as their own and Eddie Hudson, a local man who has been editor for the past seven years or so, says the aims and objectives of the *Rutland Times* remain the same as they were at its birth – to provide the Rutland community with news and views from their own area. 'The popularity of the *Rutland Times* is due in no small measure to the people of Rutland who make, supply and buy the news,' says the editor.

Writing in the first edition of the *Rutland Times* in 1977, the then local MP, Kenneth Lewis, said: 'Those who come to Rutland will see a vast lake, many pretty villages, small but thriving towns; but, more importantly, they will get the sense of community working and living together.' Seventeen years later the same words are just as applicable.

...lose
vice they now expect, and get, from most multiple outlets.
"One trader even reports that 35per cent of business last Friday came after 5pm."

Some traders however are reluctant to stay open, and

...added. "If local people see that the town's shopkeepers are unwilling to offer this service they will soon get the message that they do not wish to compete with other shopping centres. They will vote with their feet, and take their custom elsewhere."

week's Times

THIS week your Rutland Times is pleased to be able to mark the historic step forward to a return to independence for England's Smallest County by publishing a special eight-page supplement.
This not only celebrates the news but also, we hope, provides extensive information about the detailed background to the decision, as well as giving guidelines on where we go from here.

MAGIC!

Rutland in line for full county

...E is now on for Rutland to forge a ...pendence. The Local Government ...as we predicted a month ago, has ...d that Britain's Smallest County be ...the magic word 'county' came over ...r in the Commission's re ...that if the proposals are ...en Rutland WILL becon ...that implies.

Try that for size

REBECCA Trenwith, a Year 10 pupil at Uppingham Community College, will be putting her best foot forward on Wednesday when she

Rutland

meml

Rutland ⌂ Times

Issue No. 289   Friday, December 3, 1993

RUTLAND NEWS FROM COVER TO COV

MISSING COUPLE MYSTERY

BODIES FOUND

...over. Two bodies were
...e from the couple's bun-
...ing.

...ch team during the latest
...o after the couple were

...ce experts were called to
...detectives that the grave

...iled examination of the

...ortem examinations are
...ath.

...ded in custody awaiting
...other (69) on a day unk-

Rutland ⌂ Times

...GHT-PAGE SPECIAL CELEBRATION SUPPLEMENT

NDEPENDENCE:

ow it's
up to
OU

Co
con
cas

A PAIR
glib line
appare
juring t
tism h
Rutlan
week.
The m
Arabs,
Moroc
former
walked
post of
told p
Sheila
"going
and w
Britisl
with sp
bers 'fo
Mrs
bemuse
she beg
"If tl
fuse me
good j
was like
a bad d
on TV
believe
The
as sud
arrive
money
"I ju
this da
Mrs Ca
The
visited
Hart h
on the
pulled
once a
with ar
of cash
The
smartly
"magic
and
pin-st
were b
ing a 2
Grana

COMMUNITY

Frost in Rutland

Above: All white in the early morning, naked trees suddenly developed a white cloak near the lodge on the outskirts of Exton

No doubt about it, Mother Nature employs a very accomplished artist in Jack Frost. Just now and again the chilly character gives an outstanding exhibition of his work. This was the case recently in Rutland and *Rutland Times* editor, Eddie Hudson, went out with his camera to record these natural works of art before the wintry sunshine wiped the countryside canvas clean.

Above: Even an ordinary piece of sheep netting can be made beautiful when mist combines with a sharp drop in temperature

Right: Beech tree with an icing sugar dusting by a lane near Empingham

Above: 'May blossom' in mid-winter. This blackthorn tree was at Empingham

Left: Frosty reception which brought gasps of admiration. Looking out over Rutland Water from Barnsdale

COMMUNITY

There was a small county named Rutland...

A competition run in 1993 ended with John Barber of Oakham being crowned 'Rutland's King of Limericks'. Here are a few of the local limericks which were entered in the contest...

John Barber

A daring young fellow from Brooke
Took a girl to a sun-dappled nook.
When she cried 'No you don't!'
He said 'Right then I won't,
I'd forgotten your vicious right hook.'

A silly young fellow from Stretton
Once dressed himself up as a Breton;
He said 'If I hike
Or go on my bike,
I'll sell all my onions in Ketton.'

An angler who lived near Stoke Dry
And tried to catch fish with a fly
Said 'I've striven all night
And I've not had a bite,
So it's now Rutland Water I'll try.'

An agile young fellow from Wing
Thought he'd try out the new Highland Fling,
But, as his kilt tilted
The girl he had jilted
Said 'What a fuss over such a small thing.'

A daring young fellow from Brooke
Thought that he had what it took,
Til his girlfriend from Pilton,
And her cousin from Tilton
Said 'It's not just the size, it's the look'

Said an ugly young fellow from Ryhall
'Folks always make fun of my dial;
From all that one hears
It's the size of my ears
That induces the public to smile'.

**Sketches by
J R H Prophet.
Above: Ryhall
Right: Brooke
Far right: Wing**

Exton Street Market

Photograph R Adams

The Fair in Cutts Close during the Oakham Festival

Photograph R Adams

Music man at Rutland Water Show

Photograph R Adams

A relaxing Sunday afternoon in Cutts Close

Photograph R Adams

Rutland Youth Band at the Oakham Festival

Photograph R Adams

Wednesday Market

Photograph Brian and Elizabeth Nicholls

COMMUNITY

People in Action

People are the essence of Rutland. We may extol the scenery and villages but it is the close-knit community on which this patriotic county is based. People know each other, they recognise faces. They meet together in Market Place, in Cutts Close, at village fetes and at the now famous Oakham Festival.

Value Rutland: from small beginnings...

Rutland Passports were launched in 1993 on the front cover of the Rutland Times and with posters in shop windows.

W hen eight Rutland traders got together in the autumn of 1992 to bemoan the effects of the recession on the county's shops, they didn't realise what they were starting.

Calling themselves the 'Value Rutland Group', they set about creating a poster campaign which would stir Rutlanders into shopping locally... and gain wider publicity to bring people in from elsewhere.

Within a couple of weeks they had a success on their hands: a campaign to decorate shops throughout the county with red, white and blue posters which literally appeared overnight. The posters, which read 'Value Rutland – buy here' were paid for by the shops who used them. Each donated a few pounds to cover printing costs.

The poster campaign resulted in newspaper, television and radio reports nationwide about how England's

Some of the Rutland Passports entered in the competition, with stamps from shops throughout the county.

smallest county was fighting to beat the recession.

The following year, 1993, saw the campaign develop further. The Value Rutland Group came up with a competition based on a 'Rutland Passport' with a big prize – a holiday in Rutland, Vermont, USA. The *Rutland Times* team were persuaded to back the campaign, paying for the printing of 15,000 Rutland Passports and giving the whole of their front cover to the event. Sales of the newspaper boomed.

During the three-month competition, 'border guards' (dressed in costumes loaned by the RATS drama group) patrolled the streets each week demanding to see Rutland Passports and offering spot prizes. Shops declared their participation in the campaign with posters in windows. Newsletters from the Value Rutland Group kept shopkeepers informed of events.

Local MP Alan Duncan was photographed being hauled off by Border Guards for shopping in Uppingham without a Rutland Passport. Weekly reports in local newspapers detailed prize winners. A border control post was set up on the old A47 for a publicity stunt resulting in yet more newspaper, television and radio reports.

Sponsorship came pouring in from all directions: major donors were Ruddles, Rutland Plastics, CS Ellis Group and Arnold Wills, but dozens of others gave meals in restaurants, shopping vouchers and everything

from a watch to wool for knitting a sweater.

Over in the USA, Rutland Vermont's Chamber of Trade took the idea on board and they arranged more sponsorship. Hotel rooms, restaurant meals, car hire, day trips and souvenirs were all donated by traders fascinated with the competition.

Winner of the competition was Oakham resident David Loveday. With his wife and two young children David enjoyed the holiday of a lifetime. The family were declared Rutland's official ambassadors and were feted everywhere they went.

At the end of the campaign the Value Rutland Group discovered sponsorship had been so generous that they had made a profit. Keeping some money back for future campaigns, they agreed with sponsors to donate the majority to the newly formed Rutland Tourism Association which was created to encourage visitors to England's smallest traditional county. But that's another story.

Above: Shop windows throughout Rutland were plastered with posters in 1994 in anticipation of Rutland's return to county status.

Below: Rutland Tourism Association was launched in 1993 and soon produced both a guide to the county and a 'Where to Stay' booklet.

Helping the fight for independence

● In 1994, when Rutland's twenty-year fight for a return to county status was recognised by local government commissioners, the Value Rutland Group leapt into action once again. Within ten minutes of the commissioners' official announcement recommending Rutland's return to 'unitary status' more posters, this time in Rutland's traditional colours of golden yellow and green, covered shops, offices and houses throughout the county. They declared 'Welcome back Rutland' and 'There'll always be a Rutland'.

● With the Value Rutland Group around, Rutland is always in the public eye, confirming its long-held status as England's smallest traditional county, with a special place in the hearts of English people.

Below: Following the success of the Rutland Passport competition local business The Rutland Design Company produced a superior version as a souvenir of the old county for sale to locals and visitors alike.

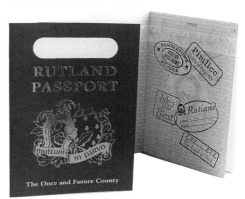

Sarah Linden and Bev Craven, Rutland Design Co

Ruddles in Rutland

The Ruddles Brewery in Langham is famous throughout the land for brewing traditional English Ales. Despite its growth from being a small, rural industry in the late 19th century, the dedication to excellence in brewing has remained unchanged.

Ruddles Langham Landmarks

■ **1841** Two maltsters in the village – Richard Thorpe and William Towell

■ **1858** Langham Brewery built by Richard Westbrook Baker

■ **1861** Inherited by Edward G Baker, son of the above

■ **1876** Owned by George Harrison, Leicester

■ **By 1881** Owned by Boys & Style, Leicester

■ **1895-1911** Owned by Henry H Parry. George Ruddle manager from 1896

■ **1911** Bought by George Ruddle for £19,500

■ **1924** Kenneth Ruddle, son of George, takes over. Tony Ruddle joins 1959

■ **1973** Sir Kenneth Ruddle becomes first President of the Company. Tony Ruddle becomes Managing Director & Chairman. Expansion from local to national markets

■ **1978** Sale of 'tied' houses

■ **1980** Ruddles County wins award for best cask beer in the country

■ **1986** Bought by Grand Metropolitan and later Courage

■ **1992** Company taken over by Dutch Brewer, Grolsch

Left: An early photograph of Langham Brewery. Note the name H H Parry

Below: Early transport at Ruddles

Historic scene in the cellars at Ruddles

Photographs by courtesy of Ruddles

101

HISTORY

·····························

The World we have Lost

Going, going, gone?

David Millard

Bryan Waites

Burley-on-the-Hill Smithy

1905
Published by Valentine Series, Dundee

This smithy was once thought to be the subject of Longfellow's poem *The Village Blacksmith*. It was also featured on a *Cherry Blossom* boot polish advertisement in the 1920s.

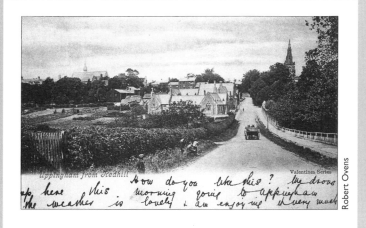

Robert Ovens

THE HERMITAGE. BURLEY WOOD

Andrew Jenkins

Uppingham from Redhill

1905
Published by Valentine Series, Dundee

The southern entrance to Uppingham ascends Scale Hill to the west of St Peter and St Paul's Church. The buildings on the left comprise the National School and Uppingham Improvement Society. They were all demolished in 1974.

The Hermitage

1910
Published by W E Exton, Oakham

This folly summerhouse constructed of tree trunks, branches and thatch with mosaic floor stood in woods near Burley House. It was burnt down in 1960.

Normanton Hall

1908 Published by Dolby Bros., Stamford

Built for Sir Gilbert Heathcote between 1733 and 1740, Normanton Hall was situated on what is now the shore of Rutland Water. The house was demolished in 1926, but St Matthew's Church and the stable block were left standing. The church was converted into a Water Museum after Rutland Water was flooded and the stable block is now Normanton Park Hotel.

Andrew Jenkins

Tickencote Hall

1911
Published by Taylor and Downs, Peterborough

Built by Sir John Vanburgh in 1705 for the Wingfield family, this fine house was sadly pulled down in the 1950s.

Andrew Jenkins

Top Road, Ridlington

Circa 1915
Published by Stocks, Uppingham

A tranquil view of Top Road and the village green at Ridlington. Note the various modes of transport – an early motor car, a bicycle, a horse and cart, and a man with a wheelbarrow. 78 years later there is little change in this view apart from extensions to the cottages and growth of vegetation, particularly the oak tree on the green.

Andrew Jenkins

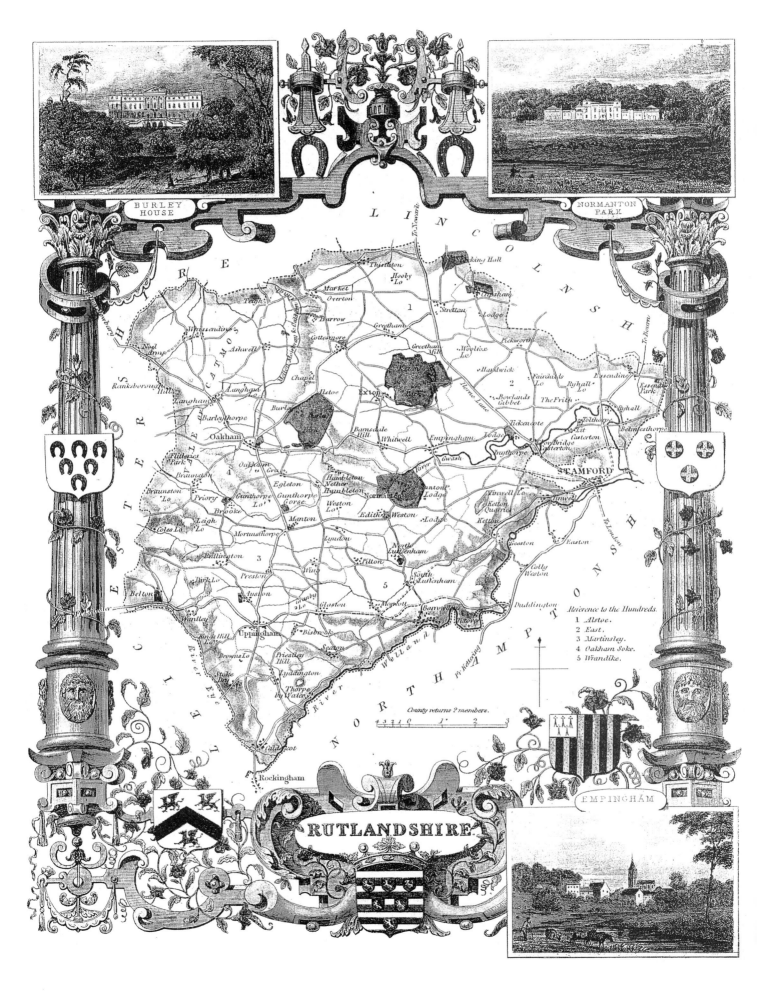

ARTS

Antique Rutland

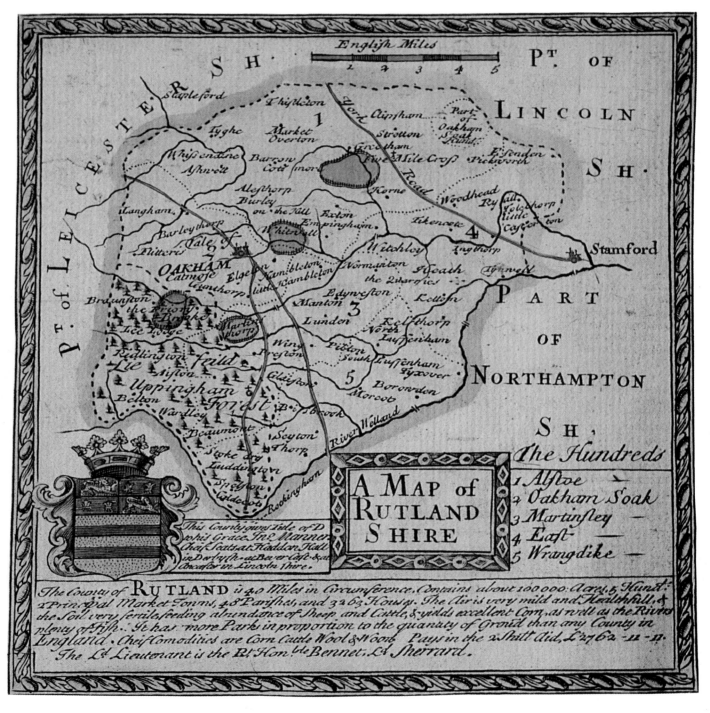

Old Rutland is attractively displayed in Antique Maps. Thomas Moule's map of 1830 is shown opposite. Above is E. Bowen's map of 1720.

Gone, but not

Part of a painted glass window which used to be in the parlour of Newnham Paddox, Warwickshire, the Feilding family seat.

Nichols - History of Leicestershire

The motto on the Rutland Coat of Arms, 'Multum in Parvo', means 'much in little' and it is equally applicable to Martinsthorpe, one of its smallest parishes. The humps and hollows of the deserted medieval village and the abandoned farmhouse at its centre, lie on a ridge between the River Chater and the River Gwash, about a mile and a quarter due west of Manton. They convey to the passer-by very little of its varied and mysterious past.

Martinsthorpe is named after St. Martin and "thorpe" indicates a daughter settlement, probably of Preston. The earliest reference to the village is in 1199 but there may have been a settlement here before the Domesday Survey in 1086. Martinsthorpe was populated by ploughmen in the medieval period and their ridge and furrow can still be seen.

The de Montfort family held Martinsthorpe as tenants of the Earls of Warwick and they sublet it to the de Seytons in the early part of the 13th century. Surviving records give some indication as to the population of the village. For example in 1327 fourteen householders were taxed. Fifty years later thirty nine people paid poll tax. By 1440 Martinsthorpe was inherited by the Feildings when William married Agnes de Seyton. At this time the village was already declining because arable land was being turned over to pasture for sheep farming.

By 1522 Martinsthorpe was virtually deserted.

SS/RO

Left: Old Hall Farm in 1993. George Cox erected the iron fence, and planted the coppice behind Old Hall Farm in the 1930s.

Below: Martinsthorpe from the north west in 1993 showing the abandoned farmhouse known as Old Hall Farm and some of the earthworks.

SS/RO

forgotten

© Crown Copyright

A bridleway from Manton through Martinsthorpe to America Lodge follows the line of an old carriage road.

Right: A 1953 aerial photograph of Martinsthorpe, looking west.

Right: Part of Ogilby's 1675 strip map of the route from London to Oakham showing the Earl of Denbigh's seat at Martinsthorpe.

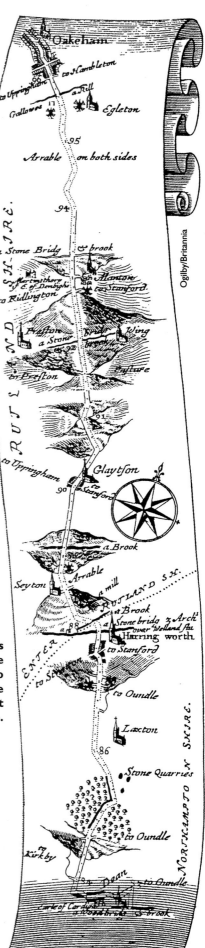

Ogilby/Britannia

© Crown copyright 1993 / MOD reproduced with the permission of the Controller of HMSO

Martinsthorpe House by Geoffrey R. Herickx. This water colour was commissioned by the authors in 1993. It is based on an engraving of Martinsthorpe House and a photograph taken by W. Stocks circa 1900 of the St. Martin's chapel ruins. Additional detail was obtained from a study of Kirby Hall near Corby which was built just before Martinsthorpe House. Although the Hall is on a more lavish scale, there are many architectural similarities, including the 'crossbow' windows, the high basement, the use of cut limestone blocks (ashlar) for external wall facing and the careful attention to symmetry.

Martinsthorpe House

About 1622 a later William Feilding built Martinsthorpe House probably as a country retreat. It was a magnificent mansion set within a park. William's brother-in-law was the Duke of Buckingham, and it was through this connection that he rose in favour at the Court of James I to become the first Earl of Denbigh. The house was used by the Denbighs until the 1670s.

The Denbighs rented out the land at Martinsthorpe and during the 17th century the Burneby family of Manton held the major part. Rent rolls show that Martinsthorpe House and Park were let to Charles Morris in 1686 and 1687. Richard Burneby and his family may have moved into the House in 1687. After 1715 the House was probably rented by Henry Green. Martinsthorpe manor was sold in 1720 and it passed into the ownership of the Duke of Devonshire before 1758. When Martinsthorpe House was demolished in 1755 it is believed that the stables were retained and converted into a tenant's house which was then occupied by the Green family. Today, this house is known as Old Hall Farm.

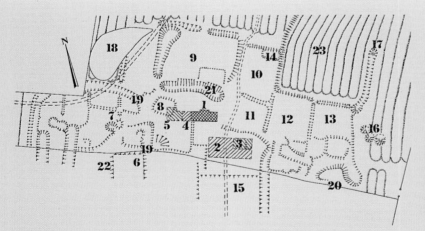

Transactions of the Leicestershire Archaeological and History Society

Plan of Martinsthorpe earthworks based on a survey by John Wacher in 1960.

St. Martin's Chapel was originally part of Martinsthorpe House. After the sale of the House the chapel was used by the vicars of Uppingham and Wing for baptisms and marriages between 1728 and 1746. When the house was demolished the chapel was left standing and re-roofed, but by 1818 it resembled an old barn. In 1885 the roof was blown off and by 1910 nothing remained. During the first half of this century the old handwritten bible from the chapel was kept in the sitting room of Old Hall Farm.

Key 1 Old Hall Farm. **2** Site of Martinsthorpe House. **3** Site of St. Martin's Chapel. **4** Site of barn demolished in 1965. **5** Site of earlier barn or stables. **6** Site of 1960 excavations **7** House platforms. **8** Possible site of Church. **9** Possible Manorial site. **10, 11, 12** and **13** Village closes. **14** Pond. **15** Site of terraced gardens to Martinsthorpe House. **16** Quarries. **17** Spring. **18** Coppice planted in the 1930s. **19** Hollow way. **20** Iron fence erected in the 1930s. **21** Possible moat. **22** Earthworks below the fence have been ploughed out. **23**- Ridge and furrow. The limited site excavations carried out in 1960 revealed structural evidence of medieval and 17th century buildings. The artefacts found are now located in Rutland County Museum. Some were of 12th century origin.

Dick Cox

George Cox and his family pose for a photograph in the front garden of Old Hall Farm circa 1928.

The Chapel

Leicestershire Museums, Arts and Records Service

Uppingham School Archives

An anonymous pen, ink and wash drawing of St. Martin's Chapel circa 1790. The crenellated wall which originally enclosed Martinsthorpe House and its garden was still standing then and it is also shown on an 1803 estate map. By 1839, however, most of it had been demolished and the stone was probably used to repair the park wall.

Andrew Jenkins

Above: Watercolour of St. Martin's Chapel and Old Hall Farm in 1839. Attributed to Alicia Wilkins, niece of the then Rector of Wing.

Left: St. Martin's Chapel in ruins circa 1900. From an old postcard by W. Stocks of Uppingham. Old Hall Farm can be seen in the background.

The west end of the present house has at some time been converted from a kitchen into a stable. The massive stepped chimneybreast and inglenook fireplace remain together with the two early 17th century bread ovens shown here.
Above right: Old Hall Farm from the south west in 1949.

Left: In 1947 a range was installed for the farm's new occupants. The bread oven in the wall to the left of this picture is of a much later date than those in the stable. To the right of the range is a brick built copper which was used for heating water. The stone arch over the inglenook is late 18th century.

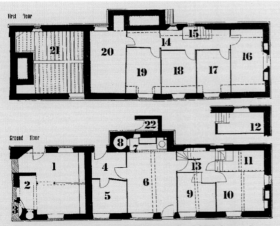

Floor plans of Old Hall Farm in 1970 based on drawings prepared by Peter Ellis.

Key 1 Stable. 2 Stable Inglenook. 3 Stable Bread Ovens. 4 Scullery. 5 Bathroom. 6 Kitchen. 7 Inglenook. 8 Bread Oven. 9 Larder. 10 Sitting Room. 11 Store Room. 12 Half Cellar. 13 Passage. 14 Landing. 15 Stairs. 16 Bedroom one. 17 Bedroom two. 18 Box Room. 19 Bedroom three. 20 Bedroom four. 21 Hay Loft. 22 Outside Toilet.

Old Hall Farm

Parish Registers, the 1841 to 1891 Census Returns, local Directories and previous residents are sources of information about the shepherding families who lived at Old Hall Farm. By 1818 the converted stables, known to be reduced in size, had become the home of James and Mary Payn. The Knowles family were the next occupants. The first detailed census shows that William Smith, his wife Ruth and their six children were living at Martinsthorpe in 1841.

After the Smith family left, the Bransons moved into Old Hall Farm. They lived there until about 1910. The farm then became the home of Mr and Mrs Sherard Reeve before the Cox family moved in during 1922. George Cox's family spent many happy years at Old Hall Farm before leaving in 1944. Three years later Herbert Gudyer, his wife and two children took up residence. They were the last family to occupy the farmhouse and left in 1950.

In 1808 ownership of Martinsthorpe passed from the Duke of Devonshire to George Watson of Glaston and then to his niece, Catherine, who married Sir William de Capell Brooke of Market Harborough. It remained in this family until 1918 when it was sold to Mr A.M. Bradshaw of Oakham. Part of the estate was sold to Richard Bradley in 1925 and in 1927 the

Arthur Branson, Margaret Stubbs (nee Gudyer), Dick Cox and Dorothy Gudyer. A nostalgic return visit to Martinsthorpe for former residents in 1993.

remainder was acquired by Col. Heathcote of Manton. The Haywood family of Gunthorpe Hall now own most of the parish.

Old Hall Farm is a handsome ironstone building with a Collyweston slate roof. It has seen several major structural changes in its long life. An estate map of 1803 shows that the building used to be twice its present length. By the end of the 19th century a barn had replaced the western half and this in turn was demolished in 1965. The present building has many interesting internal features and determining its exact history is an intriguing exercise.

There is far more to Martinsthorpe than meets the eye. Further excavations, a detailed survey of the house and additional research of old documents should reveal more of its history.

Text and compilation by Robert Ovens and Sheila Sleath

Penny Richardson

ARTS

....

An Artist in Exton

P enny Richardson has painting in
her blood. Her mother trained to
teach art and Penny naturally took
to the same gift. She lives in Exton and
paints mainly in gouache, watercolour
and oils. She started with portraits of
family pets, then horses, and horses in
landscape. She is also expert in child
and adult portraiture. With husband,
John, they also run a conservation
framing service using the purest
materials. They are Rutlanders through
and through.

**The three
illustrations
here are
paintings by
Penny.**

Photograph by John Richardson

> "
> *Sketching, painting and recording the English landscape, I realise now, is all I ever really wanted to do... I know every field, tree and shrub within a two mile radius of my studio.*
> "
>
> **Alan Oliver**

Alan Oliver's

Market Overton Church

Pilton Church

Morcott

Rutland

Alan Oliver's studio is at Great Casterton. Since 1976 he has had numerous exhibitions of his work in addition to his *Sketchbook of English Landscapes* (Sycamore Press 1985) and *Sketchbook of Rutland* (Acorn Press 1992).

The day Thou gavest...
Preston Church at Evensong

The sun dips low,
Capturing the dreaming church,
Encircling it with glow
Of radiant gold.
The steeple gleams
And blossoms, burnished bright
As if with Heavenly beams.

Make me to shine
With grace of Inner Light I pray,
My dross to gold refine.
So let Thy dawn
Dispel my night,
Eternal Sun, whose power
Envelops men with light.

Kathleen McKinnon

Barrowden Church

Wings

Fly, wild geese, fly!

Like miniature planes through the rose-grey sky,

Your rhythmic wings, wind-wheezing,sighing,

With honking, melancholy, high-pitched crying,

Wandering voices, like lost souls in flight

Cleaving the gathering gloom of the night,

Just visible,skimming the distant hill,

Eerily, mistily, calling still,

Stirring the sombre within my breast

That seeks and yearns, rejecting rest

And the questions probe,

Who am I?

Why?

But no answers echo the rose-grey sky,

Fly, wild geese, fly!

Kathleen McKinnon

ARTS

·····················

Rutland in Miniature

"

Nature and Art in this together suit,
What is most grand is always most minute

"

William Blake

South Luffenham

Our Lane, Belton-in-Rutland

How dare they christen you Littleworth? You glisten
with priceless jewels.

Consider the snowdrops, fair maids of
February, greeting, welcoming travellers from
the A47, braving the harsh winter winds,
grouping together like nuns with heads
bowed in prayer.

Then the clustering daffodils,
embroidery of brilliant gold, making our
grass verges glow with cheerfulness and
lifting the spirits of all those who gaze.

It is when the year sweetens that we
know you are at your loveliest. Exquisite
tracery of delicately perfumed elder blossom
sways and a forest of cow parsley (kek) lines
your banks like white sentinels on guard. May
blossom explodes. The breeze gently sings its
summer song as countless birds harmonise to
serenade the butterflies that float like little rainbows
from flower to flower in an ecstasy of abundance. Old, old
trees, lime and ash, spread their protecting arms, around, shielding us
from wind, the melody of your rustling leaves soothing as a lullaby.

Field Road near Belton

When Autumn comes, you still have joys to offer. How splendid
your dying leaves of gold and crimson, orange and brown, as they
scamper along, tumbling like acrobatic clowns until they embrace,
then part to go their separate ways. The elderberries droop dark,
purple-black fruit. Blackberries weave amongst the hawthorn bushes.
Jim's damson tree bends low with luscious ripeness.

On winter nights you rest quietly, calm, still, lit by your two
electric eyes and the occasional headlamps of a passing
car. The jagged outline of Harry's holly tree, her
berries already reddened scarlet, shows stark
against the yellow light. In the bungalow
beside the hen house, John and Kendal
sleep secure. You slumber, shrouded in
mystery and deep peace, whilst
friendly ghosts wander familiar haunts
on Wardley Hill.

Kathleen McKinnon

Country Lane near Belton

**These miniatures
have been painted by
Sharon Broome who
lives at Belton-in-
Rutland. Her work is
shown at actual size.**

Rutland August 1990

Oh joyous Summer's Heaven sent days
With sun drenched fields, where sheep do graze
In sweetest calm, while all is still,
As clouds drift slowly o'er the hill
Like Eider-Down, in pure blue sky.
Now butterflies flit lightly by,
And bees buzz busily around
The scented blossoms that abound.

I watch with wonder and delight
The Swallow and the Lark in flight
Soar high, above the gentle breeze
Caressing the pollens in the trees
To fill the air with somnolent scent,
As cuckoo's chant their sad lament.

Come share with me, oh share with me
This beauty of tranquillity
And fill your life, for one brief hour
With Rutland's beauty, strength, and power.

For soon the Sun will cease to shine
As we her sons, all lost in time.

Gerald Botteley

Lyddington   oil seed rape

MDW Fortschritt E517, Seaton. Watercolour

ARTS
....

Rigby
Graham in
Rutland

**Oil Seed Rape
– Lyddington.
Watercolour**

Wardley Hill in October – from our patio

A grey mist creeping
Slowly shutters the pastoral scene,
The sheep just visible on the hill
Seem indifferent, grazing still.

There is a beauty
In this melancholy monotone,
A quiet, brooding interlude in time,
Mysterious, rare, sublime.

I, too, grow quiet,
Hushed by this noiseless, floating haze;
Anaesthetizing stress and strain,
Creating space to think again.

Kathleen McKinnon

Rigby Graham is 'heir to the long tradition of English landscape painting' but he has absorbed tradition and enriched it. His 'tireless vigour and penetrating eye' extends to etchings, woodcuts, lithographs, oils, watercolours and gouaches. Yet he is an artist 'not easily classified'. Based in Leicester, he is internationally renowned and his work is frequently to be seen at the Goldmark Gallery, Uppingham.

Wardley. Watercolour

Rigby Graham: Book Illustrator

Oakham Canal ruined building

O ver a twenty five year period, commencing in the early 1960s I was closely involved with Rigby Graham in the production of more than 100 illustrated books. Some of the books carried superb drawings and coloured illustrations depicting interesting views of Rutland.

Seen through the eyes of an artist who picked out features that most people would miss and certainly the camera could not record. Dramatic, often controversial, these illustrations printed in books, now rare collectors items, record features in Rutland that in many instances have disappeared and are a contribution to the wealth of information that is available to the collector of Rutland books and ephemera.

Ruined Farm, Pickworth

In addition to illustrations published in books, Rigby has provided numerous drawings, water colours and paintings depicting Rutland scenes. Of the published books five spring readily to mind. *The Pickworth Fragment* 1966, *The Oakham Canal* 1968, *Peter Jackson* 1974, *Seriatum* 1978 and *Leicestershire* 1980.

Of the five publications undoubtedly *The Pickworth Fragment* is the most unusual.

Unquestionably the finest book the Brewhouse Press ever produced, small in size, large in format when opened, 14 feet long! Finished on Shrove Tuesday 1966, the print sequence covers the ruined village of Pickworth in the mid-1960's.

The main illustrations are progressive lino cuts showing the Pickworth arch and farm buildings. The most dramatic print is undoubtedly the firing of the lime kiln at Pickworth, which compliments Clare's 'Elegy on the Ruins of Pickworth, Rutlandshire'.

Text by Trevor Hickman

Near Pick'orth stands a long-cold kiln
Where stone once turned to lime
And where a sweating countryman
Oft turned his thoughts to rhyme.

The gentle vale, the birdsong sweet,
The common sights, and rare,
Supplied the words which flowed with ease
From that countryman – John Clare.

The world has turned oft times since then,
Thro' turmoil, pain and strife;
Yet the lime man's burning words shine through
– A country view of life.

Eddie Hudson

Near Pilton, Watercolour

Storm clouds over Cemetery Chapel Oakham

ARTS

Storm over Rutland

❝

But, if this life is all we'll know
Throughout the vast expanse of time,
And we but share, just for a while
The wonders of this human form
From that brief moment when we're born
Until the hour we breathe our last;
How much more sacred would life be?

❞

From Heaven on Earth?
by Gerald Botteley

The storm broke suddenly

The storm, not unexpectedly,
Broke suddenly
Over 3pm's picnic things;
Things ruinable such as -
Cake, and cheese sandwiches,
A nicely embroidered sunhat from Eastbourne,
Sally's new doll
And
An Agatha Christie paperback.

Tempers, frail as roses
Best displayed in a vase indoors,
Cursed the rain and ran.

Over by the hedge
Inconsequential weeds
Rocked and danced in the rain;
Tender as tissue,
Tougher than tablecloth,
Meadowsweet is built
To take storms,
And to grow lovelier by them.

Philip Ennis

Photograph by Richard Adams

119

The Tempest

Romeo and Juliet

Below: Theatregoers enjoy a picnic in the grounds of Elizabethan Tolethorpe Hall before a performance.

As you like it

ARTS

Shakespeare in Rutland

The Stamford Shakespeare Company was founded in 1968 by its Artistic Director, Jean Harley, to stage open air Shakespeare productions each summer in the Monastery Garden of the town's George Hotel. Originally the idea was to raise money for the proposed Stamford Arts Centre.

Success lead to success. Although the Company has retained its amateur status it has gained a deserved reputation for the quality and professionalism of its presentations.

In 1976, because of a rebuilding programme, the George Hotel could no longer offer the use of the Monastery Garden and the Shakespeare Company was forced to seek a new home. By chance, Tolethorpe Hall came onto the market, just two miles over the border in Rutland. A local businessman generously offered an interest free loan (since repaid) to enable the Company to buy the Hall and its seven acres of grounds for £26,000.

The Hall was derelict and the grounds overgrown. Between March and May 1977, members worked frantically to restore the property for the two plays that were already in preparation for that season. The formal gardens were rediscovered, the interior of the Hall redecorated and car parks prepared. The main task was to build the tiered auditorium in a natural amphitheatre in the grounds.

The open air theatre provided comfortable seating for 382 patrons and a specially designed canvas canopy protected the audience from the weather. After 16 years, in 1993, a new permanent canopy in high tensile fabric was built and seat capacity increased to 600.

The stage is in the open, set among a background of trees and shrubs. Full theatre lighting is used after dark and combined with back lighting through the greenery creates spectacular and colourful settings.

A bar and dining facilities for pre-performance meals add to the enjoyment of this exciting theatre. The gardens provide ideal picnic areas.

The Company's high standards are achieved through imaginative productions and intensive rehearsals. Productions are noted not only for the standard of acting but for the quality and design of costumes, props and settings.

From small beginnings the audiences have grown to 32,000 people each season. People come from far and wide. The East Midlands Tourist Board regard the performances and Tolethorpe Hall as an important tourist attraction and promote the season in Europe and North America. In 1992, the Stamford Shakespeare Company was chosen as the 'Middle England Visitor Attraction of the Year' for the high standard of facilities and its plays.

The Merchant of Venice

ARTS

Poetic Rutland

Throughout the book there have been contributions from Rutland poets. In this section some of their work is displayed together with sketches by local artists. Of the poets, Gerald Botteley and John Crossley live in Oakham; Philip Ennis in Uppingham and Kathleen McKinnon, Belton-in-Rutland. Each of them has written widely for newspapers and magazines. Additionally, John Crossley has published *Questions about Seabirds*; Philip Ennis is well-known for his series *Rutland Rides* and *Startled into Wonder*. Kathleen, who is a professional freelance poet, has published *Quiet Ways, Inner Garden* and *Hidden Fragrance*. The sketches are by David Millard, David Carlin, Anna Clayton, Leanne Debenham and Philip Ennis.

At Oakham Station

I watched her on the railway station,
She was young, about twenty-one,
Long, dark hair, and a face fair
And untroubled by time.
She had a baby
Shawled against the wind,
A boy, ten weeks old
(She told me later)
In one of those low, buggy chairs.
He stirred and cried,
She lifted him out and held him close,
And cradled his tiny head within her hand.
She rocked him gently to and fro
Against her body,
Whispering to him her secrets,
Bestowing comforting kisses
On his infant cheeks and brow.
The station was crowded,
But she was totally unaware
Of anything but love.
I envied her.

Kathleen McKinnon

To an Almond Tree, in Oakham Churchyard

On a bleak, grey morning,
A shaft of pale sunlight
Lit the black, waving boughs
Of the Almond Tree.

A sudden gust of wind
Frenzied delicate petals
That showered like pink snow
On the cold, damp earth.

As a shy child clinging
To the skirts of its Mother,
A jasmine bush weeps stars
Golden, at your roots.

Breath-taking Almond Tree!
Fragile, pink enchantment;
The ancient church, backcloth
To your loveliness.

I gazed, lost in wonder
And willed you to linger,
Fair bride, Spring adorning
With transient beauty.

Kathleen McKinnon

Parking Charge

Amidst the magic of the hills
My mind was filled with sweet delight
A soothing balm engulfed my soul
And I again was Nature's child.

The busy ant, the Honey Bee
The Mountain Ash and Chestnut Tree
The ferns and flowers all shared with me
Their timelessness and majesty.

And all this cost just 50p.

Gerald Botteley

The Execution of William Almond and John Holmes

The County of Rutland was famous it seems
For bringing fruition to man's hopes and dreams.
But on April the 5th, in 1813
A nightmare eclipsed its rich pastures green.

John Holmes, and Bill Almond weren't Angels, its true,
Just happy young fellows, with nothing to do.
Then one Winter's evening, when out for some Fun,
Bill burgled the Vicar, and was soon on the run.

John on the other hand, needing some Hose
Burgled John Cunnington's place of repose.
Soon they were caught, and whilst locked up in Jail,
Hoping that Christian good will would prevail,
They each made a statement in front of the Clerk
Confessing their guilt, which they signed with their mark.

To Oakham's old Castle , they were both sent for trial,
Where the Sheriff condemned them as 'Loathsome and Vile'
He said that the crimes, to which they'd confessed
Were 'Symbolic of Evil that must be suppressed.'
Then placing a black silken scarf on his head
Sentenced the pair to be hanged until dead.

For the 15th of March the Hangings he set,
But his wife, the most amiable Lady Margaret
Pleaded with him for the Hangings to wait
To give them more time to reflect on their fate.

In granting her wish, he blessed her, that she
Was so thoughtful of others in sweet charity.
So he postponed the hangings for twenty one days.
The Vicar that Sunday was loud in his praise.

In the meantime, John handed the Jailer a crown
For a barrel of ale, from the Wheatsheaf in Town.
Then plied him with drink every evening, till he
Dozed off in a stupor, then stole his spare key.

On the night of the full Moon, they planned to escape
By tearing in strips, William's long winter drape.
But just as they'd climbed to the top of the wall
The rope tore in two. So loud was their fall
That it woke up the Jailer, and alerted the Guard
Who shackled them both, then back through the yard
Of the Prison they dragged them, and hauled them inside
To be tied, stripped, and flogged till for mercy they cried.

The morn of the Hangings, crowds lined the Lea
From all over Rutland, They gathered to see
The Fiddlers, and Gypsies, and Tumblers, and Clowns,
In Carnival spirit, all over the Downs.

Whilst back in the Prison, it was quiet as the grave,
Where white faced, with lips trembling, trying to be brave,
William and John were soon on their way
With the Hangman in Black, on the top of the Dray.

The Dray slowly rumbled towards the New-Drop.
With soldiers, and Watchmen assembled to stop
Any rescue attempt, by family or friend
Of the two hapless wretches, about to descend.

*At Oakham Gallows on Monday,
April the 5th 1813 for
Burglariously breaking open the
houses of the Rev. Richard Lucas
and John Cunnington.*

They rolled on to South Street, then turned left to see
The New-Drop of Oakham, with ropes dangling free.
Then off from the cart, they were both lifted down
To mount up the steps, at the edge of the Town.

There was Booing, and Jeering, and Hissing,and Cheers,
And even the Children did join in the Sneers.
Till the Vicar in falsetto voice, did intone
A prayer for their passing, before he went home.

As the two wretched fellows, shaking with fear,
A few words did say, Contrite, and Sincere,
Around their bared necks the nooses were placed,
Then the Trap-Door burst open, their young lives to waste.

Bill's neck snapped in sunder, but John lingered on.
Black faced, with eyes bulging, he danced in the Sun
in Hideous Agony, Struggling for breath,
Writhing and Twisting, ...until Silence, then Death.

They hung there for weeks. The crows were well fed.
'As a warning to others,' The Magistrates said.
And as travellers to Oakham, passed o'er Swooning Bridge
They'd faint at the sight, at the top of the ridge.

A Broadsheet account of the Hangings reflected.
'Homes of the two, seemed a little dejected'

The remains of the New-Drop, and the Dray on which
they took their last fateful ride can still be seen in the
courtyard of Rutland County Museum. Oakham's original
Gibbet could be seen from Swooning Bridge, looking
towards Uppingham. The New-Drop however, that was
built in the early 1800s, to accommodate more than one
hanging at a time, stood at the junction of the old Stamford
Road and the Uppingham Road, about thirty yards down the
hill from South Street. It could also be clearly seen from
Swooning Bridge, but in the opposite direction.

Gerald Botteley

On Burley Hill

This is a land
Where larks lived
But not now.
A gull, alien in this upland,
Sidles across the sky,
The wind he rides
Stirring the sterile ground.

Oh yes, corn grows here
But not ebulliently
As it used to grow;
Now fluids seep in the soil
And disallow the red. the blue
The whole design which ought to be.
All sorts of interacting checks
Prevent the land from flowering.
Oh for a land possessed by larks
– they would be lifting now
on a cone of song –
And gulls going back
To a fertile sea!

John Crossley

Weather Systems . . .

. . . fuelled by
Who knows what irregularities
Hurtle over here;
Crossing with difficulty
An ocean stirred by their own violence
They explode at a touch of the shore.

There's no interruption
Where sharp winds race
Through bare woodland
And we stand
Staring down at unexpected violets;
They have crept out
In the hard, cold, spring
To use this wild light
Until leaves curtain them
In the gross obscurity of summer

Nothing we can do
Will affect or delay
The sequence that unlocks the leaves,
Do not stay out here in the cold!
Give us some sleep
Give us some alternative

John Crossley
From *Questions about Seabirds*

One O'Clock
in the Morning

The tyranny of birds is in their tongue,
Such sweet fury,
Song upon song,
Warbler, thrush and wren.
From bush and hedge,
From supermarket roof,
From paper-laden litterbins
In inner city parks,
Beaks which have stabbed
And drawn blood
Flood the vicinity
Of their victory
With undiminished song.

Their early morning carousel
Is comprehensible,
But what midnight memory haunts
The zealous nightingale
Precipitating
His nocturnal notes?
What grim exigency
Awakens him
From dreams to sing?
What glad accolade?
What salutation?

One o'clock in the morning
Is an odd time for happening.

Written after hearing nightingales in Burley Wood.

Philip Ennis

The Hawk

The hawk, determined wanderer,
Lopes up the hill.
He's no quick judge in a rage
But an inexorable cortege
Of dead dinners.

In tandem the hawk's feathers
And terror fall,
His shadow and shock
Rock
The hedges
And stir up a friction of sparrows.

He snatches but one
(One ticket's enough for a trip)
And with his luggage
Hops on to the train
Of unwearied winds
Which lug along clouds.

*Written after seeing a Sparrow Hawk take a small,
unidentified bird from the air over Galley Hill, between
Uppingham and Caldecott.*

Philip Ennis

Winter

'Midst solitude, and black despair,
The robin to the cruel night air
Does pipe sweet songs of Spring's return
In hopefulness of all things new.
With promises of greater joys
Than ever have been shared before.

More lovely will the Roses be,
And underneath the canopy
Of yonder Oak, in rainbow hue
Through shafts of light,
Like diamonds bright,
A thousand birds will come and go.
I know, for my heart tells me so.
With other wondrous, mystic things
Amongst its secret whisperings.

Gerald Botteley

A Voice for Rutland

Rutland County is my name,
Whitehall, hang your head in shame.
Leicestershire is not for me,
I have my own long history.

From towns and villages galore ,
My Rutlanders went forth to war;
Proudly they defended me
As we shared our destiny.

'Too small',cried men from London town,
High-handedly they cut me down.
My neighbour,Leicestershire, must be
Sad at such bureaucracy.

Or do men look with greedy eyes
Upon my beauty as a prize?
My shame is theirs who took such bounty;
My spirit always - Rutland County.

Rutland Times. Anonymous

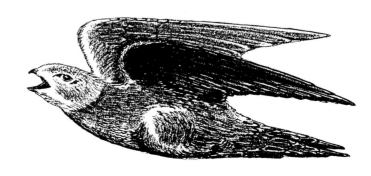

Did you know?

- Rutland became an official shire county in the 12th century.

- In 1888 Rutland became an administrative county.

- In 1894, one Urban and three Rural Districts were created operating under Rutland County Council. These were Oakham Urban and Rural, Ketton Rural and Uppingham Rural Districts.

- For 86 years from 1888 to 1974 Rutland ran its own affairs.

- In 1948 and again in 1962 attempts were made to merge the county of Rutland with its neighbours.

- In 1974 Rutland became a District of Leicestershire.

- From 1974 to the present date, Rutland District Council has provided local services under the two-tier system with Leicestershire County Council providing education, highways and social services.

- The current boundaries of the Rutland District match exactly those of the former County.

- Rutland has two towns and 53 villages.

- The area of Rutland is 150 square miles or 39,398 hectares.

- There are some 33,400 people living in Rutland. The population density of 0.82 per hectare compares with 3.50 people per hectare for Leicestershire.

- People in Rutland are more likely to live in a detached house than is the case for Leicestershire. In Rutland 44.5% of the dwellings are detached, 27.9% semi-detached and 20.9% terraced. In Leicestershire 26.2% of dwellings are detached, 37.2% semi-detached and 25.8% terraced houses. The rest of the dwellings include purpose built flats, converted property and shared dwellings.

- The proportion of rented houses is higher in Rutland than Leicestershire. Rented houses comprise 19.8% of the total in Rutland and 10.7% in Leicestershire. Owner occupied houses represent 66.5% in Rutland and 72.5% for Leicestershire. The rest of the houses are owned by the Local Authority.

- In 1971 manufacturing accounted for 19% of all jobs in Rutland, by 1981 this had risen to 36%. However in 1989 the manufacturing sector accounted for only 31.5% of all jobs.

- An estimated 948,000 visitor days per annum are spent in Rutland by tourists. Of these 50% are day visitors from Leicestershire and other parts of the East Midlands.

- Expenditure by tourism is estimated to be £13.4 million per annum, with 32% being spent by the day tourists.

- In March 1992 and March 1993 the unemployment rate in Rutland showed a favourable trend by comparison with other parts of Leicestershire. In March 1992 unemployment in Rutland was 4.1%, in Melton 5.8% and in Leicester 14.7% In March 1993 the figures for Rutland and Melton were 4.9% and 6.7% respectively, and for Leicester 15.7%

- Rutland has 537km of roads. These are made up of 42km A Trunk roads, 65km A County roads, 40km B roads 190km C roads and 200km unclassified roads.

- Daily access to the Council Offices in Oakham by public transport is available to 66.4% of the population of Rutland.

- Rutland has 57 parishes. Two more than the total of towns and villages.

- Based on the 1991 usually resident population the two largest centres of population were Oakham with 8691 and Uppingham with 3140.

- A further six parishes had a usually resident population of over 1000. The largest of these was Cottesmore with 2487. The others were Edith Weston, Ketton, Langham, Ryhall and Whissendine.

- The smallest parish In 1991 was Beaumont Chase with a usually resident population of 3. Horn, Leighfield and Pickworth all had usually resident populations of less than 20 each.

- In 1993 there were 18 Primary Schools in Rutland. The number on the roll was largest at the Oakham C.E. school with 273 pupils and smallest at Empingham C.E. with 36 puplis. The three secondary schools for pupils aged 11 to 16 at Casterton, Oakham and Uppingham had a total of 2,223 pupils in 1993. In addition Rutland has the Sixth Form College in Oakham and independent schools in Oakham and Uppingham.

Patrons

The Grolsch-Ruddles Brewing Company

Derek Penman, Barnsdale Country Club

RAF Cottesmore

Friends of All Saints' Church, Oakham

Col James Weir OBE TD DL

Pedigree Petfoods

Source: The Rutland Factfile, Rutland District Council and Dr. E Trevor Bell

Subscribers

1 Brian Montgomery, Whitwell
2 Peter John Williamson, Langham
3 Dawn Whitefield, Oakham
4 Iris V Haswell, Chester
5 Mr Charles Birch, Oakham
6 Elisabeth Howard, Uppingham
7 Mrs T E R Branson, North Luffenham
8 Mr P J K Stonehouse, Selston, Notts
9 Mrs M Griffiths, Uppingham
10 Paul Wells, Oakham
11 Jennifer M Bailey, Barrowden
12 Mr Jim Chater, Oakham
13 C H Underwood, Oakham
14 Mrs J E Hunter, Hardwicke, Glos
15 Helen Roberts, Bedford
16 Neil Forsyth, Stamford
17 Harold Killingback, Brooke
18 Bryan Waites, Oakham
19 Michael John Hinman, Coventry
20 Doreen Linton, Whissendine
21 Mrs Margaret Towl, Burley
22 Mr Michael Tolkien, Uppingham
23 Mrs Carol Debney, Greetham
24 Spaziani Graziosa, Cottesmore
25 Charles Mayhew, Oakham
26 Mrs Jacqueline Swift, Sittingbourne
27 Christopher W Jones, Preston
28 Mr Thomas Suthern, Oakham
29 Maureen Walker, Carlby
30 Roy Jones, South Witham
31 Philip Dawson, Oakham
32 Mrs D M Simmens, Thistleton
33 Dr E Trevor Bell, Oakham
34 Miss Rose Mary Fletcher, Langham
35 Mr & Mrs O'Kane, Oakham
36 Kathleen McKinnon, Belton-in-Rutland
37 Keith Richard Shillaker, Oakham
38 Mrs Julia Baxter, Eastwell
39 Mr & Mrs P C Wilson, Oakham
40 R J West, Coventry
41 J V A Long, Oakham
42 Mr & Mrs D A Iliffe, Oakham
43 Mrs A Brown, Oakham
44 Ronald B Manger, Oakham
45 Mr & Mrs V H Tomblin, Bainton
46 June & Stan Bell, Oakham
47 Margaret Tyler, Barrowden
48 Rev & Mrs D M Greenhalgh, Oakham
49 Leslie John King, Langham
50 Mrs Jean Lowe, Barrowden
51 V B English, Oakham
52 Cyril Victor Rate, Oakham
53 Mr & Mrs Brian Skevington, Oakham
54 Mrs J B Gilman, Morcott
55 Mr Cyril Greetham, North Luffenham
56 Mr Charles McIntyre, Oakham
57 Miss Pauline Mary Howard, Oakham
58 Mrs E B Barnett, Uppingham
59 Mrs Violet Lewin, Oakham
60 Marjorie Armitage, Oakham
61 Penelope Davies, Oakham
62 Ann & John Brady, Burley
63 Ronald Frederick Cooper, Oakham
64 R D West, Braunston-in-Rutland
65 K B Tidd, Oakham
66 Nigel Webb, Langham
67 Brian & Diana Glyde, Uppingham
68 J D Buchanan, Owston
69 Rev. T G Treanor, Oakham
70 Miss Sandra Skelland, Gaddesby
71 Sylvia & Michael Leach, Whissendine
72 Melissa Eden Dawson, Rugby
73 Eddie Hudson, Exton
74 Frank Harry Wolloff, Oakham
75 Frank Harry Wolloff, Oakham
76 Graham R Worrall, Barrowden
77 Mr Leslie Sisson, Oakham
78 Peter Moore, Oakham
79 Daniel M Hales, Normanton Park Hotel
80 Michael G Vecqueray, Oakham
81 Miss J M Mallett, Oakham
82 Ruth & John Edwards, Oakham
83 Professor H W Lawton, Cottesmore
84 Mrs Rhoda Johnson, Manton
85 J R Cliff, Uppingham
86 Mrs Dorothy F Dexter, North Luffenham
87 Mrs Elizabeth Boyes, Glaston
88 Mr L E Clements, Northampton
89 Mrs Hazel M Hinch, Greetham
90 Mrs A Hubbard, Langham
91 Mr H Gordon Schofield, Oakham
92 Mr & Mrs K Weatherhogg, Oakham

93 Jim Farmer, Egleton
94 Mrs P A Fagan, Royston, Herts
95 John Spencer, Oakham
96 Mr & Mrs Gerald Morley, Teigh
97 Joan & Roy Walton, Oakham
98 Martin Dolman, South Witham
99 Glynn Fisher, Pershore, Worcs
100 Dr C P Lawrence, Oakham
101 Mrs Joan Luria, Hawaii, USA
102 Alan Oliver, Great Casterton
103 Trevor Kyte, Whissendine
104 J D Buchanan, Owston
105 Mrs J F Little, Market Harborough
106 Victor Wood, Edith Weston
107 Michael John Hodges, Greetham
108 Ruth Peckover, Huntingdon
109 Mrs Irene Kettle, Exton
110 James H Barringer, Oakham
111 Edmund John Dry, Oakham
112 Mrs V R Terry, Oakham
113 Mrs Margaret Rowson, Oakham
114 Robin Baines, Oakham
115 Colin & Eileen Trundle, Stamford
116 Ted & Pat Hudson, Oakham
117 Dave Hatton, Whissendine
118 Mrs A Gilks, Braunston-in-Rutland
119 Mr J R T Hopper, Langham
120 Robbi Watson, Lyddington
121 Mrs M Hart, Whissendine
122 Mrs Beryl M Peasgood, Burley
123 W B Williamson, Holton-le-Clay, Lincs
124 Mr B C Bailey, Oakham
125 Mrs Doreen Robinson, Oakham
126 Rev & Mrs K.P.Lingard, Glaston
127 Mr & Mrs D.G.Gunn, Barrow
128 Mr Alistair L Lawrence, Oakham
129 Mrs Audrey M Buxton, Greetham
130 Mrs T C Connolly, Ketton
131 Mrs B W Clark , Oakham
132 Mrs Norton-Fagge, Preston
133 Mr & Mrs Michael Stevens, Oakham
134 Mrs Jane Stevens, Cranleigh, Surrey
135 Mr A W Burns, Oakham
136 Mrs A H Powell, Oakham
137 Mr & Mrs Colin Wright, South Luffenham
138 W Tibbert, Oakham
139 Brenda & Bill Lawson, Lyndon
140 T C Swinfen, Exton
141 T C Swinfen, Exton
142 T C Swinfen, Exton
143 T C Swinfen, Exton
144 Miss Georgina Duffin, Langham
145 Miss Elsie M Pearse
146 Mrs Angela Tyers, Oakham
147 Mrs R Richardson, Lyddington
148 H & B M Palmer, Oakham
149 H W J & A Rutland, Oakham
150 Mrs & Mrs David Partner, Oakham
151 Daniel K.George, West Ayton, Yorks
152 Louise & William Stafford, Glaston
153 Mrs W M Stokes, Normanton
154 Nicholas Steele, Oakham
155 Jill & Geoffrey Last , Ketton
156 Mrs Marilyn Nicholls, Oakham
157 Robert F Ovens, Ullesthorpe, Leics
158 Miss Sheila A Sleath, Leicester
159 Mrs Carole Brown, Bourne, Lincs
160 Penelope Loveday, Oakham
161 Mr David M Wakerley, Bisbrooke
162 John & Ann Thomson, Wing
163 Mrs Honoria Holmes, Stamford
164 Mr & Mrs J G Wilson, Oakham
165 Mr & Mrs J Grey, Rhu, Dunbartonshire
166 Mr Philip J Rudkin, Stamford
167 Gee & Bridget Tyler, Cottesmore
168 G H Boy l e, Bisbrooke
169 Mrs M D A Purdy, Oakham
170 Mrs Maureen Hollands, Ashford, Middx
171 Thomas Northen, Wilmslow, Cheshire
172 Elizabeth Northen, Oakham
173 Mrs V Adam, Oakham
174 Mrs Winifred Avison, Ketton
175 Rutland Sixth Form College, Oakham
176 David Perry, Bisbrooke
177 Dr J D S Goodman, Offham, Kent
178 Mrs Marie Eayrs, Brooke
179 Mr and Mrs R P Braithwaite, Langham
180 Suzanne & Martin Jeffery, Oakham
181 Mrs E Gilmore, Oakham
182 Mr & Mrs T E Walton, Oakham
183 James R Smith, Oakham
184 Robin Parsons, Tunbridge Wells, Kent

185 Mrs G M Ross, Oakham
186 Mr & Mrs R Dexter, Lyndon
187 Derek & Phyllis Green, Oakham
188 Mrs Ann Taylor, Oakham
189 B J & J M Stewart, Oakham
190 Laurence Howard, Whissendine
191 Mr & Mrs R Hall, Bisbrooke
192 Joan Platt, Stretton
193 Terence Arthur Burrows, Ryhall
194 Francis & Angela Humphreys, Oakham
195 Sam & Jane Stafford, Exton
196 A J & E Green, Oakham
197 Roger & Sandra Green, Langham
198 Liz Hollis, Langham
199 Mr & Mrs D Gregg, Oakham
200 Mr G McCormack, Preston
201 Mr & Mrs A E Ball, Oakham
202 Mr & Mrs Pete & Eileen Case,
    Woodhouse Eaves, Leics
203 Mrs Norah Senior, Empingham
204 Mr P R Green, Crewe, Cheshire
205 J A Mills, Empingham
206 Mr M J Bentley, Oakham
207 Sir Clifford Boulton, Lyddington
208 Rev Bernard & Mrs Margaret Taylor,
    Lyddington
209 Alec & Caroline Crombie, Uppingham
210 Mrs Geoffrey Webb, Oakham
211 Mr Keith Suthern, Solihull
212 Mr & Mrs Jim Bradley, Langham
213 Mrs L M Warwick, Stamford
214 Sharon Broome, Belton-in-Rutland
215 Mr A Ross, Belton-in-Rut land
216 Mr Mark S Green, Great Missenden, Bucks
217 Trisha Findlay, Oakham
218 Roy & Diana Strickland, Oakham
219 Mrs Brenda M Jerrome, Bristol
220 Mrs Margaret A Hallam, Oakham
221 Wilfred J Chamberlain, Benfleet, Essex
222 Dr & Mrs I McIntosh, Red Deer, Canada
223 Lincolnshire County Library Service
224 C E John Aston, Leicester
225 Squadron Leader J P Smith RAF,
    Dhahran, Saudi Arabia
226 Mrs F M Smith
227 Miss D C Smith
228 Miss M A Smith
229 Mrs K Doyle
230 Roger & Auriol Chandler, Stretton
231 Mrs M J Meatyard, Oakham
232 Mr R K Brown, Blandford Forum, Dorset
233 R Naylor, Oakham
234 G W Kirk, Langham
235 Mr & Mrs M S Hardy, Oakham
236 Mrs M Johns, Oakham
237 Mr M J Huggins, Melton Mowbray
238 Mrs Sheila Bembridge, Exton
239 Mr A B Northen, Thorpe-by-Water
240 Mrs E B Northen, Thorpe-by-Water
241 Mrs M J Fisher, Empingham
242 Mr & Mrs Joseph McGregor, Oakham
243 Miss J P Spencer, Braunston-in-Rutland
244 Don Clements, Whissendine
245 Mr & Mrs W P Bunney, Tinwell
246 Mr Ron Bullimore, Stamford
247 Mr Colin J Stuart, Uppingham
248 Mrs Jean Locke, Andover,Hants
249 Mrs S G Perry, Oakham
250 Mr & Mrs John L Knew, Belton-in-Rutland
251 Mrs Vivienne D.Cutting, Ratby, Leics
252 J H E Bayfield, Uppingham
253 Mr Keith R Berridge, North Luffenham
254 Mrs Christine Doyle, Leicester
255 Dora & Michael Pooley,Oakham
256 Mrs Joyce Butchart, Uppingham
257 Ernest & Sheila Stainsby, Uppingham
258 Lorraine Butchart & Tony Hudson, Bristol
259 Ivy Titchard,Uppingham
260 Scott & Gloria McLeod, Uppingham
261 Mrs J Tredinnick,Oakham
262 A Cox, Oakham
263 Julian Woolford
264 Clint Thelwas
265 Arthur R Branson, North Luffenham
266 Arthur R Branson
267 Mrs S E Bridge, Letchworth, Herts
268 Anthony John Cragg, Oakham
269 Mrs Molly Lewis, Oakham
270 Mary Musson Spence, Oakham
271 Mrs M Stubbs, Ketton
272 Mrs H Gudyer, North Luffenham
273 Miss Sheila A Sleath, Leicester

274 Miss M Sharp, North Luffenham
275 Mr & Mrs James E Ovens, Oakham
276 William J B Clifford, Ryhall
277 Mrs Barbara Fraser-Brunner, Exton.
278 Mr & Mrs D Parker, Stamford
279 Paula Rachel Donaldson, Hambleton
280 Mr & Mrs J R Bolton, North Luffenham
281 John D Leefe OBE, Stretton
282 P S Mann,Whissendine
283 R Green, Langham
284 Elaine Jones, Uppingham
285 Hambleton Hall Hotel
286 Arthur Lawrence, Newark
287 Fiona Canning, Newark
288 Janice & Alan Patient, Cottesmore
289 Mr Keith S McConnell, Whissendine
290 Mrs I G Davis, Oakham
291 Mrs P A Rees, Oakham
292 Mrs R Wantock, Wilmslow, Cheshire
293 Mrs F Murton, Jersey
294 Mr & Mrs T C G Rees, Oakham
295 Don & Olga Canning, Whissendine
296 N Miller, Hambleton
297 Mrs K Bonney, Oakham
298 Rev & Mrs Parks, Ontario, Canada
299 Bob & Joyce Lucas, Oakham
300 Kathleen Nicholls, Stretton
301 Mrs Sybil Hainsworth,Langham
302 Alan & Jean Wright, Uppingham
303 Marjorie Boys, Oakham
304 D J Forbes, Edith Weston
305 Mrs Margaret Wightman, Uppingham
306 Mr & Mrs R H Harvey, Great Easton
307 Kingston & Mary Smith, North Witham,
    Lincs
308 C C Burton, Empingham
309 Mrs D Robinson, Oakham
310 P N Lane, Uppingham
311 J F Gammell, Seaton
312 Mr Eric Kaljuvee, Pickworth
313 Mr G P Wyatt, South Luffenham
314 G F Wilson, Felixtowe, Suffolk
315 Mrs Jean Dumford, Uppingham
316 Mrs P M Dalby, Uppingham
317 David & Pat Roome, Ridlington
318 Paul Rowntree, York
319 Rodney & Tuk Hubbard, Ewell, Surrey
320 Michael Stafford, Atherstone, Warws
321 E F Foster Budworth, St Albans, Herts
322 Major Alexander Greenwood, Nanoose
    Bay, Canada
323 S D Veazey, Luton,Beds
324 Mr C W Cragg, Evesham, Worcs
325 Mr Richard M Hartley, Amersham, Bucks
326 T W Badgery, Upper Longdon, Staffs
327 Roberta & David Harvey Joyce,
    Market Overton
328 Mrs M E Fuggle, Oakham
329 J H Southwell, Melton Mowbray
330 Joe & Eileen Elliott, Ashwell
331 Mr & Mrs K Toon, Uppingham
332 B W Barnett, Sark, Channel Isles
333 Gerry & Yvonne Neild, Oakham
334 Mr R M Bradley, Delta BC, Canada
335-345 Leicestershire County Council
346 Mrs Ruth Watchorn, Oakham
347 Hilda & John Townsend, Whissendine
348 Mrs G Stafford, Exton
349 Mr & Mrs M Seaton, Castor, Cambs
350 Mr A Saunders, Gretton, Corby
351 Barbara Hodge, Leicester
352 Peter Tovey, Markfield, Leics
353 Mr Norman Hyde, Uppingham
354 Mr & Mrs Harold Sleath, Belton-in Rutland
355 Major & Mrs J M Ellingworth,Oakham
356 Sir Kenneth Lewis,Preston
357 Sir Kenneth Lewis, Preston
358 Michael Iannantuoni, Cottesmore
359 P E May, Oakham
360 George H Sellars, Greetham
361 L Worrall, Barrowden
362 L Worrall, Barrowden
363 L Worrall, Barrowden
364 L Worrall, Barrowden
365 Vic & Margaret Walker, Market Overton
366 Mr & Mrs G Boyall, Uppingham
367 Mr & Mrs Richard R Davies, Whissendine
368 Mrs J A Goddard, Oakham
369 S M Brand, Allexton
370 Mr John Grimmer, Oakham
371 Albert Edward Cowling, Oakham
372 Andrew Jenkins, Stamford

373 J Smith, Oakham
374 Beryl Hoy, Oakham
375 Mrs Mary Salvage, Luton, Beds
376 J M Meredith, Bisbrooke
377 Mrs M Hand, South Luffenham
378 Mr & Mrs J D Cooper, Leicester
379 J G Heron, Baldock, Herts
380 A E Land Uppingham
381 George & Kath Barron, Ryhall
382 Brian Needham, Oakham
383 Sylvia Hammond, Oakham
384 Mrs H Lee, Cottesmore
385 Martin R Eayrs, Buenos Aires, Argentina
386 Rutland Times, Oakham
387 Mr P S Brydson, Melton Mowbray
388 Fraser David Foster Farren, Oakham
389 Lewis Alexander Foster Farren, Oakham
390 Mrs Bessie Blake, Oakham
391 David A Follows, Uppingham
392 Karen Duggan, Oakham
393 Leicester Pulse Magazine
394 Anne-Marie Evans, Market Overton
395 Dr Donn Evans, Market Overton
396 Mr M Whyton, Enfield, Middx
397 E B Franks, Sleaford, Lincs
398 Mrs W P Saunders, Oakham
399 Mr Irvine Cushing, Oakham
400 I A Brayn-Smith, Langham
401 Mrs Margaret Haynes, Cottesmore
402 Mr Malcolm Paul Callun, Oakham
403 Miss Pamela Blake, North Luffenham
404 Mrs Jennifer W Ward, Whissendine
405 Edward Duncan Franks, Grays, Essex
406 Miss Beatrice Johnson, Peterborough
407 Rev K H & Mrs Wayne, East Leake, Leics
408 Mr Francis Powell, King's Lynn, Norfolk
409 Mr Francis Powell, King's Lynn, Norfolk
410 Michael G Richardson, Oakham
411 Mr T Wilks, Market Overton
412 Mr T Wilks, Market Overton
413 Mr T Wilks, Market Overton
414 Peter Smith, Whissendine
415 Spiritual Assembly of the Bahai of Rutland
416 Mr J C D Clarkson, Newton Abbot, Devon
417 Mr Edward G Leigh-Brown, Stamford
418 Uppingham School Archives
419 H H B Spry-Leverton,
    Uppingham School Library
420 Mr & Mrs J P Rudman, Uppingham
421 Mr A H Cherry, Bisbrooke
422 Mr A T Hand, Uppingham
423 Mrs Phillips, Oakham
424 Mrs Joan Cleghorn, Langham
425 Mrs D C Cassady, Greetham
426 Keith & Brenda Gibson, Whissendine
427 Caroline Rosario, Whissendine
428 Mrs Karen Brealy, Herne Bay, Kent
429 Col T C S Haywood, Gunthorpe
430 Mrs A J Griffin, Uppingham
431 Mrs B Lemon, Barleythorpe
432 J & C Beadman, Braunston-in-Rutland
433 Rutland Design Co, Oakham
434 Miss P Burroughes, Ketton
435 Mr Margaret Dickinson, Uppingham
436 Mr Norman Smith, Clipsham
437 David Millhouse, Oakham
438 Mr & Mrs D R Healey, South Witham
439 Mrs J M Stapleton, South Luffenham
440 Barbara St Claire, Stamford
441 Mrs Noreen Ansell, Wymondham, Leics
442 Anthony John Wright, Langham
443 Barrie Holland, Stoke Dry
444 E M Dorman, Bisbrooke
445 Leonard John Darnell, Oakham
446 Graham & Diane Thomas, Oakham
447 S P Carpenter, Oakham
448 Mrs Madeleine Ockwell, Ingoldsby, Lincs
449 Mrs Pamela Gamblin, Ketton
450 Dr & Mrs S B Wakerley, Clipsham
451 Geoffrey Charles Houghton, Caldecott
452 Mrs J Combe, Oakham
453 John William Robinson, Oakham
454 Mr Winston E Clarke, Melton Mowbray
455 H P Liquorish, Uppingham
456 Mr & Mrs J M Clinton, Uppingham
457 Lilian & Bill Steele, Oakham
458 Mrs M Goodrick, Oakham
459 Terence Weeden, Hornchurch, Essex
460 Sir David Davenport Handley, Clipsham
461 W T Elsworth, Oakham
462 Mr Ian Kellam, Cottesmore
463 Mr Joseph Arthur Goddard, Oakham
464 Mr Norman Thorpe, Melton Mowbray
465 Mr K Cheeseman, Ashwell
466 Lady Ruddle, Langham
467 Mrs M Catchpole, Oakham
468 Martin Downs, Ketton
469 John Downs, Ketton

470 Mrs Myra Lois Dewhurst, Leamington Spa,
    Warks
471 Mrs Pamela Hasler, Whissendine
472 Squadron Leader N V O P Healey,
    Penrith, Cumbria
473 Terence Michael Draper, Eastbourne
474 Mrs E P Garbett, Barrowden
475 Mr & Mrs H C Fairey, Oakham
476 Marilyn Pile, Leicester
477 Mr D O W Wallace, Cottesmore
478 D L & A Kanter, Wardley
479 John Edward Dixie, Ketton
480 Mr & Mrs David Williams, Oakham
481 The Common Room, Eltham College,
    London
482 Bill Taylor & Hazel Scott, Oakham
483 Mr N S Ager, Ketton
484 Mr & Mrs A E Badley, Uppingham
485 Gordon W Greenhill, Uppingham
486 Mrs Jenny Harris, Oakham
487 I M White, Ridlington
488 Mrs Barbara A Burnish, Whissendine
489 Mrs Kathleen Hill, Barleythorpe
490 Mary Davidson, Caldecott
491 Mrs E K H Miles, Pettswood, Kent
492 Nola Thurlow, Uffington, Lincs
493 Mr Trevor Archer, Whissendine
494 Nora Freeman, Oakham
495 Mrs Cann, Crawley, W Sussex
496 Miss A Badley, Stafford, Staffs
497 Mrs H Allison, Ketton
498 Mr Thomas Burrows, Ketton
499 R V Edwards, Oakham
500 Eric & Shirley McGregor, Oakham
501 David Goodrick, Oakham
502 Trevor Hickman, Wymondham, Leics
503 Mrs Sheila Hay, Brentwood, Essex
504 Mrs I A Rose, North Luffenham
505 Mr & Mrs J G Skipper, Cottesmore
506 Mrs L M Lane, Market Overton
507 Robin David Toy, Cottesmore
508 L O Smith, Cottesmore
509 Miss Joan Cramp, Oakham
510 Mr Frank Critchley, Cottesmore
511 D S Watson, Market Overton
512 R L Black, Teigh
513 Peggy Jennings, Oakham
514 T Bateman, Teigh
515 Jane Munday, Oakham
516 Vincent Munday, Oakham
517 Dick Matthews, Gunthorpe
518 Mrs N E Eley, Uppingham
519 Mrs Anne Eley, Pilton
520 Walter Geoffrey Pool, Pilton
521 Charles N Tuck, Whissendine
522 Mrs C A Harwood, Cottesmore
523 Mrs E Dolman, South Luffenham
524 Mrs Sheila Dugmore, Whissendine
525 Mr Peter Golden, Bisbrooke
526 Mrs J Page, Oakham
527 Mrs J E Coleman, Braunston-in-Rutland
528 Allan M Patterson, Oakham
529 Rachel Jones, Market Overton
530 Mr & Mrs I Taylor, Oakham
531 Mr Norman James, Oakham
532 A J Mundie, Oakham
533 Janet & Robert Smith, Bushby, Leics
534 Mr John C Pert, Manton
535 J Sutton, Ashwell
536 Angella Wiebkin-Brown, Greetham
537 Mrs Barbara Robinson, Oakham
538 Mr & Mrs J Stevens, Knutsford, Cheshire
539 George & Diane Shepherd, MarketOverton
540 Richard M Cumming, Greetham
541 Mrs Maureen Thorne, Belton-in-Rutland
542 Mr W G Lombard, Oakham
543 Mr J Horton, Queensland, Australia
544 Agnes Eleanor Taylor, Empingham
545 Mrs D M Cleave, King's Lynn, Norfolk
546 Mrs E M Rose, North Luffenham
547 Mr J Thompson, Hayes, Middx
548 Mr & Mrs Warneford Gudgeon, Oakham
549 Frances Margaret Bryan, Cottesmore
550 Anne-Marie Perks, Melton Mowbray
551 Yvonne Szymborska, Stamford
552 G P W Connelly, Oakham
553 Mrs Nancy Nicholls, Faversham, Kent
554 Michael J Norris, Uppingham
555 Mrs W M Meadwell, Oakham
556 Mr & Mrs A Edward Woolmer, Oswestry,
    Shropshire
557 Mrs Ann M Edmunds, Whissendine
558 Mrs H M S Crosher, Oakham
559 Mr & Mrs C Smith, Oakham
560 Mrs Anne Harrison, Ryhall
561 Kari J Sillanpaa, Finland
562 Mrs E Cushing, Oakham
563 K S Edward, Greetham

564 Hubert A Clayton, Horsham, Sussex
565 A Tilke, Oakham School
566 Jack & Joyce Haywood, Billesdon
567 Mrs V M Geary, Billesdon
568 Mr Alfred Smith, Cottesmore
569 Mrs B Townsend, Cottesmore
570 A Whyard, Felixstowe, Suffolk
571 E H J Stubbings, Langham
572 Peter Duffin, Belton-in-Rutland
573 Mrs J Best, Cuckfield, West Sussex
574 Mr & Mrs R Hyde, Cottesmore
575 Peter & Jane Kinal, Oakham
576 Mrs Jill Cadd, Cottesmore
577 Mr Harold Lambert, Greetham
578 Pauline Wilkes, Easton-on-the-Hill
579 Mary & Allan Cooper, Brockworth,
    Gloucester
580 Betty Hibbitt, Empingham
581 Patricia Byrne, Empingham
582 Edith M Sims, Oakham
583 Mrs Downes, Ketton
584 Mrs Downes, Ketton
585 Mrs Downes, Ketton
586 Mrs Downes, Ketton
587 Mrs Elsie M Smith, Edton, Vale of Belvoir
588 Mrs I R R Burdett, Trowbridge, Wilts
589 Ian H S Balfour, Oakham
590 D C Orton, Oundle
591 R J Gale, Braunston-in-Rutland
592 Mrs P R Pearce, Oakham
593 John Hoskins, Hornchurch
594 Mr W N Emerson, Welwyn Garden City
595 Mrs Joyce Green, Gunthorpe
596 Irvine Cushing, Oakham
597 Mrs N Merry, Greetham
598 Joanne Ward, Oakham
599 Michael P C Davies, Ontario, Canada
600 R V Hastings-Hughes, Langham
601 W G Bryan, Chessington, Kent
602 W G Bryan, Chessington, Kent
603 Mrs Harvey, Oakham
604 Mrs Harvey, Oakham
605 Mrs Harvey, Oakham
606 Mrs Harvey, Oakham
607 Mrs Harvey, Oakham
608 Mrs Audrey Walker, Belton-in-Rutland
609 Mr & Mrs Wright, Mickleover, Derby
610 Mrs G V Pawley, Tugby
611 Raymond L Hutton, Oakham
612 Mrs Frances C Moore, Grimston
613 Guy Trezona, Exton
614 Mr & Mrs Alan Southern, Oakham
615 Mrs Z M Hollis, Cottesmore
616 Mrs R Chambers, Manton
617 Mrs C Read, Bournemouth
618 Mrs C Read, Bournemouth
619 Mrs S Smith, Nythe, Swindon
620 Mr N Millington, Greetham
621 Richard Adams, Oakham
622 Stephanie Adams, Oakham
623 Gareth Adams, Oakham
624 Miss E B Dean, Oakham
625 Mrs M Gray, Braunston-in-Rutland
626 Mrs J Abbott, Market Overton
627 Ian Balfour, Oakham
628 Mrs J Chamberlain, Cottesmore
629 Martin Boughton, Langham
630 Mr & Mrs D G Knowles, Oakham
631 Mr A A Wright, Oakham
632 Mrs S E Eaton, Langham
633 Mr J J Eaton, Langham
634 Mrs Margaret Healey, Exton
635 Mrs Margaret Purdy, Oakham
636 Mrs Vera Hamilton, Oakham
637 Irene Kettle, Exton
638 Mrs G Milligan, Langham
639 Mrs Angela Walker, Market Overton
640 Mrs Angela Walker, Market Overton
641 Mr B Bagley, Oakham
642-653 Edward Hudson, Exton
654 A J Rayner, Oakham
655 Phyllis G Cook, Stamford
656 Brian Golding, Oakham
657 Rhiannon Lucas, South Wales
658 Dr T E Harris, Market Overton
659 Mrs A Eayrs, Weaverthorpe, Yorks
660 G R Worrall, Barrowden
661 G R Worrall, Barrowden
662 Barbara O'Neill, Melton Mowbray
663 Joyce Saunders, Ryhall
664 Mrs Gliddon, Biggleswade, Beds
665 A P Louise Joyce, Market Overton
666 Nicola M J Joyce, Market Overton
667 Mr Victor Durant, Oakham
668 Roy Jackson, Collyweston
669 Trevor Jackson, Ketton
670 Michael Gee, Oakham
671 Miss N J P Ray, Uppingham

672 D J Steward, Uppingham
673 D J Steward, Uppingham
674 Mrs M Wightman, Uppingham
675 M Tween, Oakham
676 M Tween, Oakham
677 Mr & Mrs K Pine, South Luffenham
678 Christine Rawlings, Oakham
679 Mr James Southerill, Oakham
680 N L McRoberts, Ashwell
681 Mr C Miller, Oakham
682 Mrs Gwendoline Johnson, Oakham
683 Jean Margaret Eyre, Ontario, Canada
684 Mr F Palmer, Langham
685 Mr & Mrs A C Johnson, Bisbrooke
686 Mr Andrew King, Honolulu, Hawaii
687 Mrs W A Baines, Oakham
688 Sylvia Hammond, Oakham
689 George Ward, Oakham
690 Mollie & Dorothy, Oakham
691 Mrs Josephine Cowling, Oakham
692 Kim Edwards, Leeds
693 Troy & Tony Marr, Pinner
694 Ceri Edwards, Batley
695 Mr Wynn Edwards, South Wigston
696 Shirley Cooper, Oakham
697 David Murray Tocher, Oakham
698 Mrs Janet Brooks, Wandsworth
699 Mrs Jean Gurr, Stamford
700 Paul Waites, Mountsorrel
701 Camilla Lauren Coates, Old Leake, Boston
702 Oliver Adam Moutrey, Peterborough
703 Brittany Mae Dawson, Rugby
704 Mr & Mrs R P Braithwaite, Langham
705 David White, Oakham
706 Mrs D Bryan, Oakham
707 Mr & Mrs J Brereton, Uppingham
708 Mr E S Sutton, Ketton
709 Mr & Mrs M L Elkins, Oakham
710 Catherine Coltman, Newport, Salop.
711 Miss D M Clarke, South Luffenham
712 Stephen P Hulatt, Ayston
713 D Nolan, Cottesmore
714 Mrs Florence Butcher, Whissendine
715 Mrs B Hill, Oakham
716 Mrs Elizabeth Hudson, Oakham
717 Doreen Coddington, Oakham
718 Victor N Underwood, Oakham
719 M Blackwell, Hambleton
720 I Southerington, Langham
721 Mrs E L Edwards, Oakham
722 Mrs Pamela Taylor, Barrowden
723 J R & S M Beckingham, Manton
724 G R Wakerley, Great Casterton
725 Mrs Doreen Smith, Oakham
726 Olive Williamson, Oakham
727 Mr R T Rees, Downton Castle, Salop
728 Mr A D Burrows, Ketton
729 Mr A D Burrows, Ketton
730 Mr R J Gurney, Oakham
731 Mrs Barbara Walters, Clive, Canada
732 Mrs Barbara Walters, Clive, Canada
733 Ann MacLeod, Oakham
734 June Mary Sismey, Ryhall
735 Janet M Thompson, Market Harborough
736 Janet M Thompson, Market Harborough
737 B W Longstaff, Taunton
738 Janis Naylor, Gretton, Corby
739 Mrs Mary Bland, North Luffenham
740 Mrs P J Simpson
741 Mr Huntingdon, Oakham
742 Mrs N H Jones, Oakham
743 John S Palmer, Oakham
744 Anne Eckles, Florida
745 Mervyn Barwell, Market Deeping
746 Mr J P W Metcalfe, Uppingham
747 Mr & Mrs R Cowling, Exton
748 Mrs M Gwynne, Uppingham
749 Albert Beer, Barnstaple, Devon
750 Mrs A Quinn, Lyddington
751 Maureen Sievewright, Oakham
752 Sylvia M Higgs, Oakham
753 J W Whitelaw, Langham
754 P A Webster, Ketton
755 E F Rippingham, South Luffenham
756 Mr A J & Mrs M A Stevenson, Coalville